Praise for *The Call to Preach*

This book has made a profound impact on how I view communicating the timeless truth of Scripture in a post-Christian context. Thanks to Steve's good work, I am reminded daily that, unless God says something to me, I have nothing worth saying.

Carlo Serrano, PhD
Pastor and Consultant
Clarksville, TN

The Call to Preach is convicting, challenging, inspirational, and very practical with excellent examples of outstanding preaching. No matter where you are on the journey of preaching, Steve Estep's book will make you a better preacher. I wish this book had been available to me when I was starting my ministry.

Keith Wright
District Superintendent (Retired)
Church of the Nazarene

Dr. Steve Estep is a uniquely gifted preacher who proclaims the hope of real life in Jesus Christ out of a personal life deeply involved in the wide variety of experiences in which his parishioners find themselves each day. *The Call to Preach* gives both new and seasoned preachers a road map to guide any sermon safely and correctly to the heart of the congregation for challenge, conviction, consolation, and connectivity to the hope found in Jesus. I am impressed with the deeply thorough mechanics that read with such clarity that preachers of varying educational backgrounds can understand and follow to completion a good word for Jesus. I highly recommend this book for every preacher and as required reading for every student in the district course of study.

Larry Leonard
District Superintendent (Retired)
Church of the Nazarene

In my biblical exegesis courses, I often invite students to think of the study as our workshop and the pulpit, lectern, or even the conversation over coffee as the showroom, like those of the master custom furniture makers. We need not take most listeners into our workshops, but we must spend time and effort there ourselves if we dare to bring our sermons to any public showing. Pastor, teacher, and master preacher Steve Estep takes us into both the workshop and the public forum and guides us through the process, from the unfocused idea to the preached sermon. I wish this distillation of Dr. Estep's decades of preaching wisdom had been available when I first began to preach. Buy it; study it; ponder it; use it. You will become a better preacher.

Dr. Joseph Coleson
Professor of Old Testament (Retired)
Nazarene Theological Seminary

In *The Call to Preach,* Steve Estep provides a powerful, personal, and practical tool for preachers everywhere to experience God-honoring preparation that leads to life-changing proclamation of the good news.

Colonel Jeffrey D. Hawkins
Chaplain, United States Army
Commandant, U.S. Army Chaplain Center & School

Those who preach, or desire to do so, would do well to remember that preaching is not a task we take upon ourselves but is a life and work to which we are called. The significance and power of that call, and our love for the One who calls us, should inspire our preparation. In that spirit, Dr. Estep has accomplished two important tasks within these pages, much to our benefit. One, he provides us with the practical tools and illustrations needed for our own engagement with the text and sermon preparation. Two, and more importantly, he rekindles our passion for the call, inviting us into a preaching life that is dependent upon and empowered by the Spirit.

Dr. Doug Van Nest
Dean, School of Theology
Professor of Pastoral Ministry
Mount Vernon Nazarene University

Steve Estep is a preacher. That's not another way to say he is a pastor, although he is a fine pastor. Dr. Estep has given himself to the craft, the art, the work of being a good preacher. As his pastoral colleague on the Kansas City District for the Church of the Nazarene, I knew something of Steve's preaching and its formative impact on the healthy and growing congregation he led. His substantive experience and education, including doctoral work focused in preaching, combine to make Pastor Estep a worthy mentor to all of us who are committed to grow as preachers. *The Call to Preach* is a thorough and practical resource that pastoral preachers would be well served to study and implement. The advice here rightly begins in the essential component of God's call to preach and the preacher's passionate response to God's call. Recognizing that passion is alone insufficient for the task, however, Dr. Estep and the preachers he includes as models take us into the practical tasks of engaging text, interpreting text, interpreting our pastoral context, and structuring the speaking of the sermon in ways that, under the power of the Spirit, create imaginative and life-giving speech. I commend this labor of love to our preachers.

Dr. Jeren Rowell
President, Nazarene Theological Seminary
Kansas City, MO

The Call to Preach is more than a book about the craft of preaching; it is a book about the crafting of preachers. After years of creative and anointed preaching, Steve Estep knows it is not enough to "get up a sermon for Sunday" but that the same Holy Spirit who makes the text active and alive must also be working within the heart of the preacher. Through simple language and proven practices, *The Call to Preach* can reignite the passion and return the joy of preaching.

David A. Busic
General Superintendent
Church of the Nazarene

THE CALL TO PREACH

The Art of Sermon Preparation

STEVE ESTEP

THE FOUNDRY
PUBLISHING

Copyright © 2018 by Steve Estep
The Foundry Publishing
PO Box 419527
Kansas City, MO 64141
thefoundrypublishing.com

978-0-8341-3753-0

All rights reserved. No part of this publication may be reproduced, stored in a retrieval system, or transmitted in any form or by any means—for example, electronic, photocopy, recording—without the prior written permission of the publisher. The only exception is brief quotations in printed reviews.

Cover Design: Glen Edelstein
Interior Design: Sharon Page

Library of Congress Cataloging-in-Publication Data
Names: Estep, Steve, 1969- author.
Title: The call to preach : the art of sermon preparation / Steve Estep.
Description: Kansas City, MO : Foundry Publishing, 2018. | Includes bibliographical references.
Identifiers: LCCN 2018041791 | ISBN 9780834137530 (pbk.)
Subjects: LCSH: Preaching.
Classification: LCC BV4211.3 .E88 2018 | DDC 251/.01—dc23
LC record available at https://lccn.loc.gov/2018041791

All Scripture quotations, unless indicated, are taken from The *Holy Bible: New International Version*® (NIV®). Copyright © 1973, 1978, 1984, 2011 by Biblica, Inc.™ Used by permission of Zondervan. All rights reserved worldwide. www.zondervan.com.

Scripture quotations marked (MSG) are taken from *The Message*. Copyright © 1993, 1994, 1995, 1996, 2000, 2001, 2002. Used by permission of NavPress Publishing Group.

Scripture quotations marked (NRSV) are taken from the New Revised Standard Version Bible, copyright © 1989 the Division of Christian Education of the National Council of the Churches of Christ in the United States of America. Used by permission. All rights reserved.

Scripture quotations marked (BSB) are taken from The Holy Bible, Berean Study Bible, BSB. Copyright ©2016, 2018 by Bible Hub. Used by Permission. All Rights Reserved Worldwide.

Scripture quotations marked (ESV) are taken from the ESV® Bible (The Holy Bible, English Standard Version®). ESV® Text Edition: 2016. Copyright © 2001 by Crossway, a publishing ministry of Good News Publishers. The ESV® text has been reproduced in cooperation with and by permission of Good News Publishers. Unauthorized reproduction of this publication is prohibited. All rights reserved. The Holy Bible, English Standard Version (ESV) is adapted from the Revised Standard Version of the Bible, copyright Division of Christian Education of the National Council of the Churches of Christ in the U.S.A. All rights reserved.

Scripture quotations marked (NLT) are taken from *Holy Bible*, New Living Translation, copyright © 1996, 2004, 2015 by Tyndale House Foundation. Used by permission of Tyndale House Publishers, Inc., Carol Stream, Illinois 60188. All rights reserved.

Scripture quotations marked (KJV) are taken from the 1987 printing of the *King James Version* of the Holy Bible, which is in the public domain in the United States.

Scripture quotations marked (NASB) are taken from the NEW AMERICAN STANDARD BIBLE®, Copyright © 1960, 1962, 1963, 1968, 1971, 1972, 1973, 1975, 1977, 1995 by The Lockman Foundation. Used by permission.

The internet addresses, email addresses, and phone numbers in this book are accurate at the time of publication. They are provided as a resource. The Foundry Publishing does not endorse them or vouch for their content or permanence.

CONTENTS

Acknowledgments	7
Part 1: The Call to Preach Is the Call to Prepare	**9**
1. Get Yourself Ready	11
2. The Call	15
3. Truths about Preaching	19
Part 2: What to Say	**33**
4. Know your Lenses and Limitations	35
Sample Sermon: Shameless, by Albert Hung	48
5. Tools for Engaging the Text: Asking the Right Questions	59
6. Tools for Engaging the Text: Initial Observations	65
7. Tools for Engaging the Text: Genre	69
8. Tools for Engaging the Text: Image of God	75
Sample Sermon: Overhearing the Regret of God, by Dan Boone	78
9. Tools for Engaging the Text: Universals in Human Experience	83
Sample Sermon: The Hope of Despair, by Shawna Songer Gaines	87
10. Tools for Engaging the Text: Bad News	93
Sample Sermon: A Communal Call to Parenting, by Robert Breddin	97
11. Tools for Engaging the Text: Good News	101
Sample Sermon: Bring It In, by Steve Estep	104
12. Tools for Engaging the Text: Points of View	109
Sample Sermon: Here's Lookin' at You, by Jeremy Byler	111
13. Tools for Engaging the Text: Desired Response	121

Sample Sermon: Go, Tell Everyone This Great News,
by Dwayne Adams   **124**

14. Tools for Engaging the Text: Congregational Blocks   **129**
   Sample Sermon: The Principal's Office, by Nancy Cantrell   **132**
15. Tools for Engaging the Text: Engaging the Senses   **139**
16. Tools for Engaging the Text: Possible Directions   **143**
17. Sermon Purpose   **149**
18. Consulting the Scholars   **153**
   Sample Sermon: Sozo, by Steve Estep   **160**
19. Consider the Context   **165**
   Sample Sermon: Love Must Be Given Away,
   by Tim Whetstone   **172**
20. Including Other Voices   **177**
   Sample Sermon: The Active Mission of Jesus,
   by Mike Jackson   **179**
21. Long-Range Planning   **183**

Afterword   **191**

ACKNOWLEDGMENTS

■ IT WOULD be impossible to acknowledge all the people who have encouraged me, taught me, invested in me, prayed for me, and contributed to my understanding of and appreciation for preaching. We are each products of the gifts God has given us in other people: mentors, teachers, friends, pastors, supporters, encouragers, and listeners.

Over the last twenty-plus years, I have served as senior pastor at three congregations: the Church of the Nazarene in Harrisonville, Missouri; Grace Church of the Nazarene in Clarksville, Tennessee; and now the First Church of the Nazarene in Marion, Ohio. All three of these congregations have encouraged my pursuit of studying and teaching preaching, and have made those pursuits possible by granting sabbaticals for study, rest, reflection, and writing. They have also been gracious in allowing me time to train the next generation of preachers through adjunct professorships, primarily at Nazarene Theological Seminary. For that I am grateful.

The staff members with whom I have worked since 2003 (when this process began) have spurred my growth as a preparer and preacher of sermons. They include Nancy Cantrell, Jimmy Skeen, Rachel Kuhn, Dwayne Adams, Zach Carpenter, Rachelle Clark, Elissa Shattuck, Bailey Bussell, Patrick Taylor, Joe Voight, Darrel Hartsock, Clayton Gregory, Hunter Hickman, Johnny Edler, Gregg Parkman, Jayme Reger, Jerry Campbell, Rob Utley, Sawyer Harlow, and Nate Laughhunn. There have been many other teachers and writers whom I view as giants in the field not only for their preaching skills but also for the consistency between their lives and their sermons. They too have helped shape my preaching life.

ACKNOWLEDGMENTS

She has often said it would be a terrible life sentence to be married to a bad preacher—for the last twenty-seven years on this wild ride of pastoral ministry, my bride, Michelle, has been my biggest encourager. She has been a sounding board and has offered insights I wish I were smart enough to think of on my own. She and our three kids, Brandon (who is now preaching himself), Brooke, and Blake, have not only served as the source of many a good sermon illustration, but they have also been the best family a thick-skinned and (hopefully) tenderhearted preacher could hope to have. I am also grateful to my siblings, Eddie Estep, Scott Estep, and Kim Duey, and my parents, Don and Joyce Estep. This family has shown me more grace than I deserve, modeled lives of Christlikeness, and shown me that the words preachers proclaim really can be embodied in real people who have a heart after God.

I also want to give a word of thanks to my editor, Audra Spiven, and The Foundry Publishing. The book you are reading is much better than the original manuscript they received. The careful attention, insightful recommendations, and gracious work made this first-time author come across much better than I would have on my own. It's been a joy to work with The Foundry Publishing on this project!

I never wanted to be a preacher. Prior to accepting the call, I wrestled with it, denied it, ignored it, and hoped it would just go away. I am so grateful to the persistent and patient God who invited me on the amazing journey of preaching ministry. Of all the people he could have chosen, I am glad he chose me! My desire has been to do him justice and bring a smile to his face. It has been my goal never to enter the pulpit ill prepared. This preparation has been more than an attempt at faithfulness; it has been an act of worship.

Part 1
THE CALL TO PREACH IS THE CALL TO PREPARE

Over time, every preacher develops his or her own process for sermon preparation. Some of these processes are more intuitive than intentional. Some approach the task like a rigorous academic effort while others lean more toward hugging an altar than holding a commentary. Some begin the process early, weeks or even a year in advance. Others aren't sure what text they're going to preach on Sunday until Saturday afternoon. Some have a full-blown manuscript and have labored over each letter. Others scribble a couple of bullet points on scratch paper a few minutes before stepping up to the pulpit.

It is my firm conviction that the call to preach is also the call to prepare. The Spirit whom we long to be at work in the proclamation is the same Spirit we very much need to be at work in the preparation. So, before we dive into talking about some of the various tools preachers can use to prepare, let's take a deeper look at why preparation matters.

one ▪ GET YOURSELF READY

*Get yourself ready! Stand up and say to them whatever I command you.
Do not be terrified by them, or I will terrify you before them.*
—Jeremiah 1:17

■ **TYPICALLY,** we prepare for meaningful moments. We care enough about significant events to invest whatever time, energy, and expense are necessary. We prepare for weddings, graduations, and other special occasions with months of planning and dozens of decisions; we recognize how much the details matter. Meaningful moments are worth the time and effort that are required to prepare for them.

We see this principle frequently in Scripture. When God was about to deliver the Israelites from four hundred years of servitude in Egypt, he told them to get ready for what he was about to do. Forty years later, when it was time for the Israelites to enter the promised land, they didn't just wake up and waltz in. Crossing over from wilderness wandering to promised-land living took preparation. Later, God sent John the Baptist to prepare the way for Jesus, and then, throughout his ministry, Jesus told parables of preparedness so that his followers would ready themselves for what was to come. After Christ's death and resurrection, Paul told the church in Corinth to get ready for Christ's return. In all these instances, we see the same idea reinforced again and again: meaningful moments require preparation.

For those who have been both blessed and burdened with the call to preach, a significant moment comes every seven days. The beauty and brutality of time is that it is predictable. If we want Sundays to be meaningful for those who come hungry to hear a word, then like Jeremiah, we must get ourselves ready.

By "get ready," I don't mean throw something together on Saturday night or download the latest free sermon series from a popular preacher. I can appreciate contemporary preachers' willingness to share their intellectual property, but the accessibility of online sermons has made plagiarism a difficult temptation for some preachers to resist. Some behave as though they can address their congregation's spiritual formation by warming up someone else's work and serving it at another table. While we can certainly benefit from other preachers' work that will "preach" in our context, we cannot neglect the work of contextualization. When God told Jeremiah to get himself ready, I don't think God meant for Jeremiah to jot down a message he'd heard from some other prophet, add his own illustration, and repeat it as though it were his own. Making ourselves ready means taking the time necessary to hear from God, not just from other preachers. It also means doing the necessary and sometimes challenging work of congregational exegesis (more on that later).

Preparing ourselves is spiritual, intellectual, and emotional work. In order to derive the energy necessary for preaching, we must first expend time, energy, and prayer in preparation.

Readiness and Routine

Do your best to present yourself to God as one approved, a worker who does not need to be ashamed and who correctly handles the word of truth.
—2 Timothy 2:15

Athletes have routines of readiness: many perform pre-game rituals, such as eating the same meal or putting on their socks in the same order before each game. While many players have their own peculiar routines, there is usually also a collective routine observed by the whole team. They do things like sit in the same seats on the bus when traveling to away games; perform their warm-up exercises at the exact same time on every game day; or tap something (like a sign, sculpture, or symbol) on their way out of the locker room. These routines are part of the ritual for preparing to play. There are parallels between Friday-night huddles at high school stadiums and Sunday-morning gatherings in church sanctuaries. Just as a team gets itself ready to play, a church gets itself ready to worship, to share life with one another, and to extend love to the world.

If we acknowledge the necessity of preparing ourselves for an event as relatively minor as a date, a game, or a weekend trip, how much more does proclaiming a word from God require preparation? Make yourself ready! These words are just as relevant for preachers today as they were for Jeremiah.

Over the last ten years, I have enjoyed teaching homiletics at the seminary, university, and course-of-study levels. I've led workshops on preaching to army chaplains, spoken at denominational events and trainings, and written blogs and articles about preaching. I have not taught the history of homiletics or the performative aspect of proclamation. I have not defined or developed a unique approach to sermon structure like Frank Thomas, Eugene Lowry, or Paul Scott Wilson. I have instead focused on an intentional approach to preparation by introducing students to a variety of tools for engaging the text. In the process, I have encouraged students to find their own systematic approach to making themselves ready.

The process I am advocating emerged at the intersection of ideas from two sources: a statement by Fred Craddock, and the words of Jesus in John 12:49–50. Craddock taught that, unless the preacher has two "aha" moments in engaging the text, the congregation is not likely to have one. Craddock means that if a message is to be effective, the preacher must have an epiphany not only about sermon content but about sermon form. His book *Preaching* presents a twofold model of preparation: interpretation and design.

Every homiletician seems to have a different definition of preaching, but I've never found one better than Eugene Peterson's translation of Jesus's words in John 12:49–50: "The Father who sent me gave me orders, told me what to say and how to say it. And I know exactly what his command produces: real and eternal life. That's all I have to say. What the Father told me, I tell you" (MSG). In this book, I seek to offer some different tools for engaging the text that, with the inspiration of the Holy Spirit, will help you hear the Father telling you what to say and how to say it.

As you read, I pray this book will spur you to consider your own method of sermon preparation. Perhaps this text will help you identify some methods you've been using intuitively and can now employ more intentionally. Perhaps it can help you articulate your own process to others—be they parishioners who wonder "how you come up with what to say on Sunday," or up-and-coming preachers looking for role models from whom they can learn. This book is the fruit of twenty-five years of preaching, countless conversations about homiletics, and the influence of great preachers, writers, and teachers who have contributed to my understanding of and appreciation for this incredible craft. Virtually everything I share I learned from someone else; my only original contribution is the synthesis and structuring of the thoughts that form my approach to the challenging, daunting, humbling, and fulfilling work of preparing to preach.

two ▪ THE CALL

■ WHY do you preach? I'm sure it's for the same reason I do: you were called. As the preacher of Hebrews writes, "One does not presume to take this honor, but takes it only when called by God, just as Aaron was" (Heb. 5:4, NRSV). While the Hebrews text is referring to priests, the idea is also applicable to all who preach. We don't presume to take this honor; we do it because we were called. In fact, we'd be crazy to do it if we weren't called because preaching is a dangerous business. Martin Luther articulated it well when he wrote, "How difficult an occupation preaching is. Indeed, to preach the Word of God is nothing less than to bring upon oneself all the furies of hell and of Satan, and therefore also of [. . .] every power of this world. It is the most dangerous kind of life to throw oneself in the way of Satan's many teeth."[1]

In *Preaching from Memory to Hope*, Thomas G. Long tells the story of Luther's first time celebrating mass as an ordained priest. Drawing on the work of biographer John M. Todd, Long writes: "A new priest's first mass was a highly public spectacle, a kind of nuptial, graduation party, and debutante ball wrapped into one. . . . As the moment approached, the 23-year-old Luther was as nervous as a groom, and unfortunately, as

---

1. Martin Luther, *D. Martin Luthers Werke: kritische Gesamtausgabe*, vol. 25 (Weimar, Germany: H. Böhlaus Nachfolger, 1902), 253. Quoted in Charles Campbell, *The Word before the Powers: An Ethic of Preaching* (Louisville: Westminster John Knox Press, 2002), 69.

Todd observes, 'The day itself proved to be, if not exactly a disaster, a day which Luther could not remember without quaking.'"[2]

Luther didn't drop the sacred bread or spill the wine—instead, he froze. He was seized by panic at the moment he was supposed to speak, and he couldn't do it. The weight of serving as a spokesperson for God hit him full force. The prior who was there to assist him turned Luther back to his task, and Luther finished the mass without the congregation noticing his moment of terror. Why would he continue to subject himself to such a traumatic experience? For the same reason you and I go to the pulpit every week: he was called to do it.

Luther never lost his wonder and terror at the prospect of preaching. Even in his later years, Luther said, "Though I am old and experienced in speaking, I tremble whenever I ascend the pulpit."[3] Reflecting on Luther's words, Stephen Farris wrote, "We indeed ought to tremble before the chutzpah of the claim that God speaks through us. If it were not for the work of the Holy Spirit, the task would truly be beyond us—light years beyond."[4]

It was a sultry August night at the West Virginia Church of the Nazarene campground in Summersville, West Virginia. Through the years, numerous kids, teens, and adults had experienced the presence of God on the sanctified grounds of that holy place. I was there that Friday night for my older brother's ordination. General Superintendent Dr. Raymond Hurn placed his hands on the head of each ordinand as a platform full of ordained elders laid their hands on them. That line of hands stretched back to the ordinations of preachers past—from Calvin to Luther, from Augustine to the apostles. Dr. Hurn's charge that night came from 2 Timothy 4:2: "Preach the word; be prepared in season and out of season."

---

2. Thomas G. Long, *Preaching from Memory to Hope* (Louisville: Westminster John Knox Press, 2009), 27–28.

3. Elizabeth Achtemeier, *Creative Preaching: Finding the Words* (Nashville: Abingdon Press, 1980), 13. Quoted in Stephen Farris, *Preaching That Matters: The Bible and Our Lives* (Louisville: Westminster John Knox Press, 1998), 7.

4. Farris, *Preaching that Matters*, 7.

Honestly, I'm not sure I heard anything after "Preach the word." Those words, and the Spirit who gave them, captured me. It was as close to God's audible voice as I've ever heard. The call was clear: I wasn't called to administrate a church, counsel the confused, chair meetings, serve on committees, mow the grass, take out the trash, or shovel a widow's driveway (although all those things often come with the territory for a pastor)! I was called to preach.

Chances are, you're reading this book because you were called to preach too. For me, that call is still as fresh as it was on that Friday night in August. As with a good marriage, time has only made it better, serving to deepen my appreciation and love for my call and for the God who issued it.

That night in Summersville, I experienced a mixture of excitement, relief, fear, and inadequacy, a reaction I later learned is common. Jeremiah couldn't see himself fulfilling the call; his response to God was, "Alas, Sovereign LORD . . . I do not know how to speak; I am too young" (1:6).

But in the face of Jeremiah's fears, God gave him what he needed: "The LORD said to me, 'Do not say, "I am too young." You must go to everyone I send you to and say whatever I command you. Do not be afraid of them, for I am with you and will rescue you,' declares the LORD. Then the LORD reached out his hand and touched my mouth and said to me, 'I have put my words in your mouth'" (vv. 7–9).

God does the same for all those he calls; he rescues us, touches us, and puts his words in our mouths. If he didn't, we couldn't preach his Word—and we would be crazy to try!

The night I told my parents about my call, my dad's first response was, "We're proud of you; all we've ever wanted is for you to know and do God's will." Then he said, "You're going to have to learn to be thick-skinned."

The preachers who have gone before us knew something about thick skin: Jeremiah was beaten and thrown into a cistern for preaching the word of God (38:1–13). Jesus was nearly thrown off a cliff after his first sermon (Luke 4:28–30). Who in their right mind would sign up for that? Well, *we* would, wouldn't we? Because we heard God's call and said yes! In the midst of the challenges and dangers we experience as preachers,

Jesus's words in John 15 resonate: "You did not choose me, but I chose you and appointed you so that you might go and bear fruit—fruit that will last" (v. 16).

We read Scripture differently after we've been called to preach. For instance, "I urge you to live a life worthy of the calling you have received" (Eph. 4:1) takes on new meaning once God has called us. Whenever and wherever you received your call, you do what you do because of it. We preach because we've been called, and the call to preach is always the call to prepare. As Dennis Kinlaw writes, "The call to preach comes not because we are worthy, but because Christ has a world to save and He has no one else to help Him in the task but you and me. When we stand in the pulpit, we must be aware of the fact that we are there by virtue of His saving power and His call to the ministry, not by any virtue of our own."[5]

Of all the methods God could have chosen, he chose to speak through prophets, poets, priests, and preachers. He is still delivering his word all over the world by means of human voices. To be chosen as one of those voices should be both terrifying and humbling. The blessing and burden of delivering a word from the Lord is great, and it demands preparation.

As preachers of the gospel, we have been entrusted with the very words of God—a high calling indeed! We are messengers, instruments, mouthpieces who need the wind and breath of the Holy Spirit if we are to speak at all. I know of no greater calling. The call to preach is the call to prepare. That is my deep belief, but it's not the only belief that informs my approach to preaching and preparation. In the next chapter, I'll share a few more convictions that are fundamental to my understanding of preaching.

---

5. Dennis Kinlaw, *Preaching in the Spirit* (Wilmore, KY: Francis Asbury Press, 2010), 48.

three ▪ TRUTHS ABOUT PREACHING

The Preacher and the Sermon Are Married

▪ AS KINLAW writes, "The greatest problem in preaching is not the preparation of the sermon but the preparation of the preacher."[1] It is impossible (or should be impossible) to separate the preacher's spiritual life from their preaching life. Before we are called to be preachers of the Word, we are called to be followers of the living Word, sons and daughters of God. Warren Wiersbe writes, "Preaching is not what we do; it's what we are. When God wants to make a preacher, he has to make the person, because *the work we do cannot be isolated from the life we live.*"[2]

Since the character of the preacher is so intimately entwined with the integrity of the message, there is no way to talk about preparing to preach without addressing the spiritual vitality of the preacher. While my view of the Word is too strong to say that the integrity of the messenger determines the effectiveness of the message (Philippians 1:15–18), I do contend that the spiritual life of the preacher will either advance or hinder the efficacy of the proclamation of the Word.

We won't be flawless in the way we live out our faith from day to day—we are human beings, after all. We will experience seasons of fatigue and dryness, seasons in which we continue to proclaim the Word

---

1. Kinlaw, *Preaching in the Spirit*, 17.
2. Warren Wiersbe, *The Art & Craft of Bible Preaching* (Grand Rapids: Zondervan, 2005), 78. Emphasis added.

even though we do not feel like it. But if we want to preach in the power of the Spirit, we have to live in the power of the Spirit.

The preparation of the preacher is spiritual work. In Acts 4, when Peter and John were brought before the Sanhedrin after healing the beggar, it was evident to everyone in the room that they spoke with an authority beyond their own: "When they saw the courage of Peter and John and realized that they were unschooled, ordinary men, they were astonished and they took note that these men had been with Jesus" (v. 13). When we spend time with Jesus, it shows.

There are many things that can hamper our preparation as preachers: hidden sin, an anemic prayer life, insufficient quality time in the Word, a lack of integrity, spiritual or physical exhaustion. Heed these words from Dan Boone: "The finest homiletical form and scholarship cannot drown out a life that is not vitally connected to the Living God. Tend your soul. Listen to God."[3] A failure to tend our own souls is unacceptable. A shallow spiritual life will result in shallow sermons that build shallow faith.

Another hindrance to preparation is relational tension—whether with God, our spouse, a parishioner, a neighbor, or even a stranger. Jesus instructs in Matthew 5:23–24, "Therefore, if you are offering your gift at the altar and there remember that your brother or sister has something against you, leave your gift there in front of the altar. First go and be reconciled to them; then come and offer your gift." And in Romans, Paul exhorts, "If it is possible, as far as it depends on you, live at peace with everyone" (12:18). We must take relational tension seriously because it can hinder not only our worship but also our proclamation.

Unfortunately, it's not always possible to resolve relational tensions prior to the preaching moment. For one thing, our attempts at resolution may be met with resistance—if you've ever seen someone sit through an entire sermon with arms crossed and jaw set, you know what I'm talking about. (And if you *don't* know, you'll probably find out at some point!)

---

3. Dan Boone, *Preaching the Story that Shapes Us* (Kansas City, MO: Beacon Hill Press of Kansas City, 2008), 189.

It's important to remember that the call to preach doesn't include the caveat, "Preach only if they like what you have to say." The call to preach is the call to make ourselves ready, and then to share what God gives us. If a tense relationship is hindering our preaching, it is our responsibility to restore that relationship (or at least attempt to do so). Conflict usually doesn't resolve on its own; someone has to take the initiative to make peace. Failure to do so not only has an adverse effect on the preaching moment, but it also taints the preparation. If, while preparing a sermon, the preacher constantly sees the face or hears the voice of someone with whom he or she is in conflict, it will inevitably come out in the tone, tenor, or content of the sermon. Like those who need a lesson in what *not* to say on social media, the preacher who refuses to resolve relational tension too often brings private conversations into the public forum—and there is no place for that in the pulpit.

I think it's safe to say that every preacher has probably experienced relational tension on a Sunday. For me, there has been more than one Sunday morning on which I've had to give a word of apology in private before proclaiming the Word of God in public. In the order of service, "passing the peace" really can provide an opportunity to pass and receive the peace of Christ that resolves relational tension.

Preparing ourselves to preach requires physical, spiritual, and emotional energy. It can be exhausting, especially when we realize how much is at stake—and how prone we are to get in the way. We must pray without ceasing and rely on God's grace to prepare our hearts so we don't preach *at* people, preach in anger, or do disservice to the gospel in our own frustration. Difficult? Absolutely! Impossible? Not with God! As J. Ellsworth Kalas writes, "The goal, in short, is for the preacher to deliver his or her soul to the people. This presupposes that the preacher will have taken proper care of that soul, so there is something worth delivering."[4]

Besides relational tension, another hindrance to proclamation is physical fatigue. Of course, there may be times when an accident, emer-

---

4. J. Ellsworth Kalas, *Preaching from the Soul: Insistent Observations on the Sacred Art* (Nashville: Abingdon Press, 2003), 17.

gency, or crisis results in a late Saturday night, and when that happens, we can trust God to give grace in the form of energy. There will be other times when Sunday comes and we are just tired from a busy week. But as a general rule, we should do our best each week to come to the preaching moment physically well prepared. With Paul we say, "To this end I labor, striving with all His energy working powerfully within me" (Colossians 1:29, BSB). I never want my preaching to suffer because I stayed up too late, didn't eat right, or failed to exercise—in other words, because I was a poor steward of the body God gave me. Come Sunday, the God who called us together with the church who gathers to hear us deserve the best we have to give.

Finally, when it comes to the Sunday message, one of the greatest gifts we can offer is our own relationship with the Lord. People should be able to tell that when we're talking about God, we're not talking about a stranger. Our congregants not only *expect* us to have an intimate personal relationship with God, but they also *need* us to—and they should be able to rely on that relationship. Barbara Brown Taylor expresses it like this: "Those who listen to us expect more than a history lesson on Luke–Acts plus some freeze-dried stories we got out of a book. They want food for their hearts. They want help for their souls. They want to see Jesus, or at least someone who knows Jesus, and God help us if we offer them less than that."[5]

Preaching is not just one of the things we do; it is intimately and intricately connected with who we are.

Preparation Takes Time

Many preachers can relate to the lyrics of Roger Murrah and Randy Van Warmer, made famous by the country band Florida Georgia Line: "I'm in a hurry to get things done/I rush and rush until life's no fun/All I really gotta do is live and die/But I'm in a hurry and don't know why."

---

5. Barbara Brown Taylor, "Preaching into the Next Millennium" in *Exilic Preaching: Testimony for Christian Exiles in an Increasingly Hostile Culture,* ed. Erskine Clarke (Harrisburg, PA: Trinity Press International, 1998), 98–99.

However, in his introductory remarks to the *Interpretation* commentary on Revelation, Eugene Boring writes, "In responsible preaching and teaching from the Bible, there can be no quick homiletical fixes, no Saturday night specials, no raiding of either the Bible or books about it [to this I would add websites or podcasts] for valuable but loosely attached items that may be attached for a quick profit."[6]

The call to preach is the call to prepare. Every once in a while, an inspired hour or two of preparation may yield a word we can't wait to deliver. But usually, it takes time—a lot of time. The more hurriedly we approach the task of discerning a divine word for Sunday, the more apt we are to take shortcuts, compromise the process, or depend on someone else more than we depend on the Spirit. Granted, it doesn't help when the Spirit seems less concerned than we are about the dwindling hours between now and Sunday—but that's all the more reason to start early. In the words of Fred Craddock, "Any doctrine of the Holy Spirit that relieves me of my work and its responsibility is plainly false."[7]

It takes time to hear from God. And people *need* us to hear from God. While our congregants may not express it in the same words, Jeremiah's flock voiced their need this way:

"Pray that the LORD your God will tell us where we should go and what we should do."

"I have heard you," replied Jeremiah the prophet. "I will certainly pray to the LORD your God as you have requested; I will tell you everything the LORD says and will keep nothing back from you."

Then they said to Jeremiah, "May the LORD be a true and faithful witness against us if we do not act in accordance with everything the LORD your God sends you to tell us. Whether it is favorable or unfavorable, we will obey the LORD our God, to whom we are sending you, so that it will go well with us, for we will obey the LORD our God."

Ten days later the word of the LORD came to Jeremiah. (42:3–7)

---

6. M. Eugene Boring, "Foreword" in *Revelation. Interpretation: A Biblical Commentary for Teaching and Preaching* (Louisville: Westminster John Knox Press, 2011), vii.

7. Fred Craddock, *Preaching* (Nashville: Abingdon Press, 1985), 30.

Ten days later Jeremiah got a word. *Ten days?* Good for you, Jeremiah, but we don't have ten days. Sunday comes every seven days, whether we're ready for it or not! Though we may fret at times, I think God knows how often Sunday comes. Not once have I had to stand before a congregation and say, "There's no word today." God is always faithful to give his people a word—and he does it through messengers who are faithful to wait, listen, pray, and speak the words he's given them.

The Source is Scripture and the Spirit

In John 15 Jesus said, "I am the vine; you are the branches. If you remain in me and I in you, you will bear much fruit; apart from me you can do nothing" (v. 5). While these words are true for every follower of Jesus, they are especially true for preachers. A constant sense of dependence on God not only keeps us humble, it also keeps us attentive, and attentiveness puts us in a position to hear from God. When we remain dependent on God, we're less tempted to imagine we came up with a great sermon on our own. Instead, we give glory to God as we remember that, if anything we said bore fruit, it was because the Vine gave us life.

Jesus the preacher announced his dependence on the Spirit when he quoted from Isaiah 61 in his first public sermon: "The Spirit of the Lord is on me, because he has anointed me to proclaim good news to the poor. He has sent me to proclaim freedom for the prisoners and recovery of sight for the blind, to set the oppressed free, to proclaim the year of the Lord's favor" (Luke 4:18–19). The Spirit anointed Jesus to *preach*. This scripture should remind us that Spirit-filled preaching has always been God's means of getting the good news to the world.

We preachers are convinced that through the public proclamation of his Word, God can and does free, heal, and enable people to experience his divine favor. Through the foolishness of preaching, relationships are reconciled, bodies healed, doubts dispelled, hearts inspired, minds transformed, and destinies changed. The source of this power is the Spirit at work in us. As Mary Catherine Hilkert writes, "Preachers, like poets and prophets, spend their lives in the dangerous company of words precisely because they are convinced of their power. Yet preachers claim more than a human craft. From the time of the Apostle Paul, Christian preachers, like the Hebrew prophets before them, have insisted that the power of preaching is the power of God (Rom. 1:16; 1 Cor. 1:18); the word they speak, God's own."[8]

People who make the effort to wake up and come to church on a day they could have slept in have certain expectations when they enter the sanctuary. Many of those expectations are directly tied to the preacher, the sermon, and the experience with the Word that will facilitate a divine encounter. They know when they get it. They know when they don't.

I was reminded of this reality when, at a restaurant near Vanderbilt University in Nashville, Tennessee, I overheard a young woman telling her friends about her recent church experiences: "This one just talked about political stuff. Another one, the sermon had no substance. I went to another where it just seemed like everyone was trying to be cool. But I guess other churches are—well, the opposite of that. I don't want to talk bad about church, but those are the things I've noticed."

I was intrigued for a number of reasons. First, I was impressed that this young woman was intent enough in her search for God that she was willing to visit multiple churches. Second, I was intrigued that her focus was not on the friendliness of the church, the level of hospitality extended to visitors, the quality of the programs, or the condition of the sanctuary; rather, her primary interest was in the sermon. She was voicing exactly what Mary Catherine Hilkert expresses in *Naming Grace*: "The 'anointing of the Spirit' that is necessary to hear the word includes a desire to hear and be challenged by the gospel. The Christian community knows when that has not happened precisely because the Spirit of God stirs up resistance and creates expectations that have not been fulfilled."[9]

---

8. Mary Catherine Hilkert, *Naming Grace: Preaching and the Sacramental Imagination* (New York: Continuum, 1997), 7. See also William H. Willimon, *Undone by Easter: Keeping Preaching Fresh* (Nashville: Abingdon Press, 2009), 30. "We preachers need a robust conviction of the Holy Spirit's work because we, unlike most academic interpreters of the Christian faith or of Scripture, must stand up and speak a word to God's people, here, now. The Holy Spirit is the power of God, empowering humanity to know God. The Holy Spirit is God's agency in preaching, that which makes sermons work."

9. Hilkert, *Naming Grace*, 85.

The community that gathers for corporate worship needs to be challenged, inspired, transformed, and liberated by a word that is true to the ancient text yet made fresh by the ever-present Spirit who works in and through it. The Spirit speaks to the preacher through the written Word, through the still, small voice, and through the voices of others. Until the Spirit speaks to us, we have nothing to say. The source of our preaching must be Scripture and the Spirit.[10]

Preachers Can't Be Pimps

No better thing can happen to our preaching than having a passionate love affair with the Bible. We suffer the burden of familiarity, and in most cases, we also suffer the burden of an education. We become too bookish about the Book, so that we see it as a source of sermons and studies, and we are more taken with the problems of scholarship than with the wonders of its continuing power. . . . We need a grand love for the Bible because it is our basic document. It is not only the particular source of our preaching, but it is also the book that so uniquely understands us, that we gain our understanding of life through it.

— *J. Ellsworth Kalas*[11]

One of my favorite phrases to share with preachers in the making is "Don't pimp the Word." What do I mean by "pimp the Word"? When we go to the text not to be wooed by it but, rather, to use it for our own purposes, we are pimping the Word. When our primary question upon approaching the text is, *What can I get out of this to give to someone else?* we are working as pimps. Of course, if we are to have anything worth sharing with the congregation, Scripture must be our source. But when we fail to approach the Word from a place of submission, and instead seek only to mine a word for someone else, we've gone from having a loving relationship with the Word to pimping it. Before we share it, we have to let it engage us.

I don't think we'll ever love proclaiming the Word if we don't love the Word we're proclaiming. Dan Boone puts it this way: "As preachers,

---

10. "The finest eloquence, the cleverest presentation, the liveliest and most up-to-date form of communication will only bear fruit if the Spirit is present." Thomas H. Troeger, *Ten Strategies for Preaching in a Multimedia Culture* (Louisville: Abingdon Press, 1996), 8.

11. Kalas, *Preaching from the Soul,* 19.

our first act of preaching is to listen with deep confidence for the breath of God moving in and through the texts that we are given to preach from. Our task is not information but revelation. And the only hope we have is the ever-present Spirit of God speaking."[12] That means we need to do much of our work without the confusion and distraction of other voices—including commentators, historians, and other preachers, no matter how knowledgeable they may be. We need the time, space, and atmosphere to engage the biblical text and hear God speak *to us* through it. His is the voice we most long to hear; we go to the text not to master it but to be mastered by it. Robert Farrar Capon advises, "Never think of yourself as 'studying the Bible.' That's for Scripture scholars, not preachers. You're supposed to be *falling in love* with the Beloved in whom you are accepted—not proving that your interest in Scripture is intellectually respectable. Even Scripture scholars (when and if they're good preachers) rarely strike that smarmy, self-congratulatory note. They always seem more smitten than smart . . ."[13]

The reality of pastoring is that the urgent can hijack the important. With all the demands of pastoral ministry,[14] we preachers can easily find ourselves overwhelmed by responsibilities, as the apostles were in Acts 6. There is always a lot to do: first-time guests to contact, hospital visits to make, couples to counsel, ball games and band concerts to attend, staff to coordinate, ministries to oversee, community organizations to engage, finances to track, leaders to train, weddings to officiate, funerals to preside over, membership classes to teach—and we haven't even mentioned time with our own families yet! Meanwhile, prayers can be left un-prayed and proclamation may suffer because in the frenzy of *doing* ministry, we forgot that the call to preach is the call to prepare. Of course, we cannot neglect

---

12. Boone, *Preaching the Story that Shapes Us*, 44.

13. Robert Farrar Capon, *The Foolishness of Preaching: Proclaiming the Gospel against the Wisdom of the World* (Grand Rapids, MI: William B. Eerdmans Publishing Company, 1998), 62.

14. The *Manual* for the Church of the Nazarene divides the massive list of responsibilities for senior pastors into two categories: core duties and administrative responsibilities. It's a long list!

the priestly work of pastoring—we would do so at our own peril. But neither can we neglect the work that is necessary to feed the flock a divine word come Sunday morning.

When the other demands of ministry detract from the kind of preparation that includes a personal encounter with Scripture and the God of Scripture, there is nothing left to do but go to the text in search of one thing: *what can I get out of this to share with someone else?* When that happens, we cease being proclaimers and instead become pimps. We use and even abuse the Word for the sake of having something to say on Sunday morning. The living, breathing, piercing, healing, convicting, consoling, and transforming Word of God wasn't intended to be pimped by ill-prepared, distracted, unable-to-balance-the-demands-of-ministry preachers who spend just enough time in it to construct a shallow sermon. Rather, the Word of God was intended to be passionately proclaimed by well-prepared preachers who shout from the rooftops what they've heard God whisper in their ears. Prioritizing our time with God so that we can hear the whisper prevents pimping the Word.

Unless God Says Something to Us, We Have Nothing Worth Saying

Then the Lord reached out his hand and touched my mouth and said to me, "I have put my words in your mouth."

—Jeremiah 1:9

There is a good reason that the *Manual* for the Church of the Nazarene lists the first two core duties of a pastor as "pray" and "preach the Word."[15] This ordering is also consistent with the primary duties determined in Acts 6: "So the Twelve gathered all the disciples together and said, 'It would not be right for us to neglect the ministry of the word of God in order to wait on tables. Brothers and sisters, choose seven men from among you who are known to be full of the Spirit and wisdom. We will turn this responsibility over to them and will give our attention to

---

15. *Church of the Nazarene Manual: 2017–2021* (Kansas City, MO: Nazarene Publishing House, 2017), 200, paragraphs 515.1, 515.2.

prayer and the ministry of the word'" (vv. 2–4). Note that Spirit-filled leadership was required for both the ministry of the Word and the service of the community. But for those who were called to preach, prayer and the study of the Word were the highest priorities. The disciples delegated other responsibilities so that those who were called to preach and teach could devote adequate focus to the task.

If our preaching is to be worth hearing, prayer and the ministry of the Word are inseparable. One cannot prepare to preach without prayer, for in prayer we hear the voice of God telling us what to say and how to say it. Several times in his Gospel, John notes that Jesus's approach to proclamation was to listen first: Jesus said what the Father told him to say. We are called to do the same. We, like Jesus, must get away from all the other voices so we can hear the Father. If we really believe that God has something to say to us and to his people, it is crucial that we carve out the time and space necessary to hear him.

It all starts with the Word. When we feel Sunday approaching at warp speed, we might be tempted to quickly refer to what others have said about the text. There is a place for that, of course—preachers who do not do the work of exegesis are asking for trouble. However, I'm advocating a process that holds the scholars at bay until the preacher has had a chance to personally encounter the text and the God of the text. We can count on God speaking to us through Scripture, but that will generally mean spending significant time in the text.

We can also expect to hear God speak through others. You've probably experienced a moment of insight that came in conversation with a parishioner, friend, family member, or even a stranger. The key is to be tuned in so that when God speaks, we recognize his voice. Until we hear from God, we won't have anything worth saying to anyone else.

Preparation Fuels Passion

There is something intangible for which every preacher longs: Some call it anointing. The old-timers called it unction. I prefer to call it passion. Passion transcends the preacher's own energy or excitement; its source is the Spirit. It flows from the preacher's soul when he or she has been truly impacted by the text and the God of the text. We know when we have it, and so do our hearers.

The congregation longs for passion just as much as we do. People can tell the difference between a passionless and passion-filled sermon. Darius Salter gets at this when he writes: "It is up to the pastor to see that there is abundant fuel. The world has the right to ministry ignited by a transcendent source. The fueling and the firing will have to be done on a daily basis. If not, it will be as disappointing as the leftovers from yesterday's breakfast. It is almost impossible to fool the guests."[16]

Passion emerges from confusion, frustration, and sometimes even despair as we wrestle, pray, meditate, and await the epiphany the Spirit brings. In that process, we hear not only what we should say to others but also what the Spirit has to say to us. And once the "aha" moment happens, passion stirs deep in our souls; like the prophet Jeremiah, we cannot contain it: "His word is in my heart like a fire, a fire shut up in my bones. I am weary of holding it in; indeed, I cannot" (20:9). Hearing from God gives us a confidence that comes not from our own abilities but from divine assurance. It gives us an ache, a hunger for the Word to work in the hearts of those who listen. Sometimes this ache brings me to tears as I study or practice a sermon out loud. Preparation imparts not only confidence to proclaim the Word but also passion from the Spirit to preach it boldly.

When we preach, we must do more than teach a set of principles. Too much contemporary preaching is comprised of nothing more than hackneyed, churchy common sense, treating Scripture like a sanctified self-help book that teaches us how to raise our kids, get along with our spouses, communicate, get promoted at work, manage our money, and find our best life now. But when Jesus came on the scene, he didn't say, "The Spirit of the Lord is on me to teach some principles that will improve people's lives." Rather, the Spirit anointed him to preach a word that would *set people free*. Maybe it's possible to get passionate about teaching principles. But when the Spirit ignites our souls with a life-transform-

---

16. Darius Salter, *Preaching as Art: Biblical Storytelling for a Media Generation* (Kansas City: Beacon Hill Press of Kansas City, 2009), 157.

ing word that does more than merely inform, the sermon becomes a very different thing: it's a word that liberates the oppressed, announces the kingdom, resurrects the dead. If we can't get passionate about that, we should probably be doing something else.

When that fire is ignited in the soul of the preacher, we allow the passion, the unction, the fire to burn with beauty, image, and language that allow it not only to be heard but also to be felt and experienced. When it happens, we find ourselves searching for the right way to say it so people will feel it like we feel it. When the passion is ignited, we may not yet know how we're going to get there, but we know where this word is taking us, and we have a drive, a deep desire, to get it said in a way that will allow that to happen for everyone who hears it. Until that fire happens, we are not ready to preach.

I don't believe it's too much to expect that kind of fire every time we preach. *Every time we preach.* It might mean earlier mornings or later nights. It might mean long, restless prayer sessions. But when we take the time that's necessary to prepare ourselves, engage the Word, and seek God, it will happen. It's important to remember that his strength is made perfect in our weakness. I'm sure we can all testify to times when we've been weak, exhausted, overwhelmed, and underprepared yet still felt the Spirit at work in our proclamation. However, those gifts of grace are not to be presumed—we do not have the option to continuously approach the pulpit unprepared. While there will be exceptions, we should seek to spend as much time as necessary in order to hear from God not only what to say but also how to say it. The call to preach is the call to prepare. Preparation takes time—and preparation fuels passion.

Part 2
WHAT TO SAY

Take a few minutes to read Acts 27. What do you see? Hear? Taste? Feel? Smell? What stands out to you? With whom do you most identify?

Much has been written about engaging the senses in preaching, but I'm asking these questions for a different reason. What we see, or fail to see, in Scripture is largely determined by our own posture, place, and preconceptions. When we come to Scripture, we all bring something with us.

If I'm in the middle of a storm myself, I see the storm in Acts 27. If I'm a pastor called to lead in a tumultuous time, I see Paul's boldness in speaking to his storm-tossed companions. If I am three or four days into a tribulation, I might notice the phrase "fourteen days" in the text.

We all have lenses through which we see the world and read Scripture. That's one of the reasons we can read a scripture we've known our whole life and suddenly see something we never saw before: we bring something to the text we didn't bring when we read it last week or preached it a year, or three, or thirty years ago. We bring a broadened experience that widens our perception, enabling us to see things that haven't stood out in prior readings.

This type of experience points to a depth of the Scriptures that can never be exhausted, but it also testifies to a depth of insight that comes from a continually maturing walk with Jesus. To say we have lenses is simply to acknowledge the reality that none of us approach the Word in a vacuum. We are all formed, informed, and influenced by a variety of factors. Our age, race, tradition, socioeconomic level, education, location, occupation, marital status—all this and more influence what we see and don't see in Scripture.

In the following chapters we will take a look at the lenses we already wear, and I'll offer you a few others to try on too, in the hope that they will provide you with some new tools with which to engage the text. You will also find some sample sermons that the Spirit breathed into being when the preachers looked through some specific lenses during their preparation.

four ▪ KNOW YOUR LENSES AND LIMITATIONS

■ "WHICH is better? One," *(click),* "or two?"

Many of us have sat in an optometrist's office, forehead pressed against a small rubber square as the doctor clicks different prescription lenses before our eyes.

"Three," *(click),* "or four?"

The optometrist works hard to ensure we get the best prescription possible to compensate for the deficiencies or distortions of our own eyes. The end goal is clear vision.

We all have lenses through which we see the world, God, the Bible, and ourselves. To say we have lenses is simply to acknowledge that none of us approach the Word in a vacuum. We are all formed, informed, and influenced by a variety of factors. Age, race, tradition, education, location, occupation, socioeconomic status—all this and more can influence what we see and fail to see in Scripture.

I once saw a church sign that said, "We don't see things as they are; we see things as we are." We can see this truth play out in history. Calvin and Wesley wore different lenses: From his legal background, Calvin saw the primary attributes of God as justice and sovereignty. Wesley certainly agreed that God is just and sovereign, but he saw the primary attributes of God as holiness and love. Different lenses lead to different insights, different observations, and ultimately, different conclusions.

As Paul said in 1 Corinthians 13, we see in part, and we know in part. The question is, do we recognize which lenses we wear and what limitations come with them?[1]

Limited Experience

The most beautiful people we have known are those who have known defeat, known suffering, known struggle, known loss, and have found their way out of the depths. These persons have an appreciation, a sensitivity, and an understanding of life that fills them with compassion, gentleness, and a deep loving concern. Beautiful people do not just happen.

—Elisabeth Kübler-Ross[2]

Throughout the years, my dad's words to me on the night I was called to preach—"You're going to have to learn to be thick-skinned"—have come to make a lot of sense. Fairly early in ministry, I learned the necessity of praying for resilience. But as I met seasoned preachers who'd developed calluses not only on their hide but also on their hearts, I began pairing my prayers for a thick skin with prayers for a tender heart. We preachers can't afford to have one without the other.

I think this gets at what God was telling Jeremiah when he said, "Get yourself ready," and then, "Do not be terrified by them." Terror at what others think can lead to a muffled voice. As those who have been called to proclaim the life-giving, sometimes difficult Word of God, we cannot afford to be muffled any more than our congregation can afford to hear a watered-down word. In *The Pastor as Minor Poet*, Craig Barnes describes this in terms of "gravitas":

> The old seminary professors used to speak about a necessary trait for pastoral ministry called gravitas. It refers to a soul that has developed enough spiritual mass to be attractive, like gravity. It makes the

---

1. "The true danger is our failure to come to terms with how the human imagination is at work in creating whatever understanding we have of life, including our biblical interpretations. When we ignore the imagination, then we run the risk of promoting a faith that is encrusted with bigotry and dogmatism unworthy of our Savior's name . . ." Troeger, *Ten Strategies*, 119.

2. Elisabeth Kübler-Ross, *Death: The Final Stage of Growth* (Upper Saddle River, NJ: Prentice-Hall, 1975).

soul appear old, but gravitas has nothing to do with age. It has everything to do with wounds that have healed well, failures that have been redeemed, sins that have been forgiven, and thorns that have settled into the flesh. These severe experiences with life expand the soul until it appears larger than the body that contains it. Then it is large enough to proclaim a holy joy, which is what makes the pastor's soul so attractive. The early church found gravitas through persecution. The desert fathers and monks found it by abandoning comfort and dedicating themselves to a vocation of prayer for the world. Most reformers have found it in prison. The American slaves found it in the hot cotton fields. Pastors find it by committing themselves to the One who called them into ministry, but whose work is so often resisted by the congregation and by the pastors themselves. Gravitas sounds difficult. It is. But the only alternative is to give up on the sacred poetry, and that's the last thing a congregation needs from its pastor. As odd as it may sound, it's the scars on a pastor's soul that make it attractive. This is also what gives credibility to the Gospel the pastor proclaims . . . Everyone knows when we're preaching from our souls and not just from the textbooks we've collected."[3]

Halfway through John's Gospel, Jesus returned to where it all started: "Jesus went back across the Jordan to the place where John had been baptizing in the early days" (10:40). Throughout my years of preaching, I've had to take many trips back to Summersville, West Virginia—back to where it all began.[4] I've kept going back because I want to hold onto the sense of awe, wonder, and terror of receiving the greatest calling under the sun: the call to preach.

When I think back to that August night nearly thirty years ago, I am embarrassed by how little life experience I had. Since preaching my first sermon, I've traveled internationally, lived in four different states, gotten married, become a father, bought houses, and completed two more

---

3. M. Craig Barnes, *The Pastor as Minor Poet: Texts and Subtexts in the Ministerial Life* (Grand Rapids, MI: William B. Eerdmans Publishing Company, 2009), 49.

4. Most of those trips were taken figuratively, but parts of this book were written there on a return visit in July 2015.

degrees. A seasoned preacher sees the text in ways a young preacher does not. This is not because a young preacher can't get insight from Scripture but because a seasoned preacher is reading from a different, hopefully deeper place.

Though today I can say I've experienced much more of life than I had back then, it is still the case that my experiences are limited, and those limited experiences create the lens through which I see the world around me and the world of the text in Scripture. This is true for all of us: A woman preacher reads a text differently than a man. A preacher in war-torn Iraq reads Scripture differently than a preacher who has never left Iowa. Anyone who's lost a child, buried a spouse, or experienced the trauma of abuse sees the text through the lenses of their own experience.

This is why, when Paul gave his charge to young Timothy, he included the instruction "endure hardship" (2 Timothy 4:5). When we endure hardship by the grace of God and emerge having been conformed that much more to the image of Christ, it serves to deepen not only our individual spiritual life but also our preaching life. Decades of preaching and pastoring will help us mature. But still, even when we're old and gray, our experiences will have been limited.

Personal Biases

When I pastored in Tennessee, a wrecker would come by every few months and drop a busted-up car at the entrance of the church parking lot. Inside, we had a classroom where adolescents heard from police officers, state troopers, and the parents of people who had been struck by drunk or distracted drivers. Out in the parking lot, we arranged orange cones into a track for golf carts. This was part of a local program for students to learn safe driving habits.

After some classroom time, students took turns driving the golf carts. Each driver was accompanied by an officer who gave them instructions: "Both hands on the wheel. Now one hand. Try to drive while you're texting but don't slow down." Inevitably, the young drivers would run over cones that represented people. The officers also brought sets of goggles that simulated different degrees of inebriation. When students put on the goggles, their vision became distorted. What they saw and what they thought they saw were two different things. The lenses made it impossible for them to see their surroundings as they really were, and such impairment affected their driving.

The lenses that can distort our reading of the gospel more than anything else are the lenses of personal bias and prejudice. These biases affect our vision of Scripture even when we are not aware of it.

What is your view of women in ministry?

Do you believe we must be strict, literal, twenty-four-hour, seven-day creationists to be orthodox Christians?

What kind of people do you picture when you hear the word "sinner"? What color are they? What nationality? What political persuasion? What language do they speak? What's their sexual orientation?

We might have biases or assumptions about Jesus, Paul, the doctrines of salvation or grace, different people groups, what it means to be human, the roles of husbands and wives, what a worship experience should include or exclude, the kind of music that can glorify God, the translation of the Bible that is most appropriate, or any number of other issues.

The lenses we wear (or that were put on us by our family or country of origin) create biases that may be more informed by the world than by Scripture. These biases and prejudices have to be addressed, forgiven, and humbly laid at the feet of Jesus if they are to be anything other than detrimental to our interpretation and proclamation of the Word.

Not convinced? Take a look at the last few sermons you've preached. Watch or read them with this question in mind: *what biases, assumptions, or prejudices came through in this sermon that I didn't recognize or intentionally include?* Typically, we prefer for a text to confirm our biases and prejudices, not challenge them. But we must become aware of this dynamic. We see in part, and we know in part.

The goal here is not a lens-less reading of Scripture—that's impossible. Instead, the goal is to understand ourselves and what we bring to the text. What biases or prejudices have become ingrained in the way we view the world? What sources have informed that? How do our lenses help or hinder our ability to see, interpret, and proclaim the Word?

Culture and Kingdom

I rarely listen to TV preachers, but on a family vacation several years ago, I turned on the TV while I was getting ready and heard a preacher shout, "The American dream is God's dream!" This preacher went on to equate the American quest for wealth with God's good will for all his children. Obviously, this preacher didn't use Scripture to interpret culture; instead, he used the greed-based consumeristic culture to interpret Scripture.

Unfortunately, we don't have to seek out a TV prosperity preacher to hear sermons that are more shaped by the culture of the world than by the kingdom Jesus proclaimed. The preacher's role is not just to be pastoral but also to be prophetic. We occupy the unique position of having one foot in the life of the congregation and the other in the life of the text. Rather than take a foot out of either one, the preacher is called to bring the world of the text to bear in the world of the congregation. In order to do this, we must be able to see both clearly. To stand solely with the text leaves the congregation without an advocate; to stand solely with the congregation leaves the text without a voice. We must know the context and culture of the Bible, as well as the context and culture of our congregation.

Pluralism is the water in which we are swimming. It's not *part* of our culture; it *is* our culture. In this climate, it's tempting to, at best, soften, or at worst, eliminate exclusive claims of an inclusive gospel. While the preaching of previous generations featured too much either/or, the temptation for preachers today is to frame everything in terms of both/and. It is dangerously easy to compromise the gospel's demands for unadulterated allegiance to Jesus, who is the Way, the Truth, and the Life. But in seeking to make Christianity more palatable, we fail to truly minister to those whose greatest need is to have their minds and hearts transformed, rather than to have their ideas reinforced.

I know I have been formed by the people who taught me. One of those people is Charles Campbell, a great preacher and thinker who wrote, "Christians learn to discern the work of the crucified and living Jesus in the midst of the powers of death when they come to see the world through the lens of Scripture, rather than interpreting the Bible according to the values and priorities of the world."[5]

Even the most sincere, committed Christ followers have biases and prejudices. One example of this is Peter's vision in Acts 10. His prejudice against gentiles ran deep; it had been formed not only by his family of origin but also by the teachings he'd heard in the synagogue, so it had become a core belief. When God showed Peter a sheet full of unclean animals being let down from heaven, Peter's initial reaction was so deeply ingrained that it came automatically. God had to launch three full-frontal assaults against Peter's prejudices before the meaning of the vision began to sink in. This stubbornness isn't because Peter was a hardened sinner or because he didn't have the heart of God. It's because Peter was a product of his environment; he perceived that his prejudices described things not only as they were but also as they should be. It took a direct intervention from God for him to change his outlook.

The call to preach does not instantly transform our sinful biases and prejudices into Christlikeness. Just like those to whom we preach, we preachers are formed and sometimes deformed by deep-seated biases, and we need nothing less than divine intervention to identify and overcome them. This is yet another reason we must submit ourselves to the text before we try to formulate something to say about it: when we approach the Bible in the right frame of mind, we open ourselves to divine revelation and redemption of our biases.

Theological Assumptions

Most denominations, associations, and independent churches see the value of trained clergy. The curriculum in my own tradition, the Church of the Nazarene, includes classes in systematic and biblical theology, church history, hermeneutics, counseling, exegesis, missions, and administration—and rightly so.[6] It is critical that those who claim to have

---

5. Charles Campbell, *The Word before the Powers: An Ethic of Preaching* (Louisville: Westminster John Knox Press, 2002), 102.

6. Still, I find it interesting that in my own tradition, a person who is called to preach can meet all the educational requirements for ordination with only one class in preaching.

a word from God be trained in doctrinal orthodoxy. That practice has always been the case; we even see it in Scripture when Paul warns Timothy, "Watch your life and doctrine closely" (1 Timothy 4:16).

Belonging to a chosen tradition has inherent dangers. I'm not saying that preachers should not be part of denominations—I myself am proud to be part of the Church of the Nazarene. But whatever tradition we come from or preach within, we need to be aware of that tradition's influence on our proclamation. For example, in the Church of the Nazarene, we do not believe that speaking in tongues is evidence of being filled with the Holy Spirit. In fact, this practice is strongly discouraged in our denomination. Consequently, when I prepare to preach from scriptures like Acts 2 or 1 Corinthians 14, I know that I am seeing these passages through the lens of my chosen tradition, which has the potential to hinder my reading and understanding.

The same can be said for someone coming from a Reformed tradition when it comes to texts like 2 Peter 3:17–18. A theological conviction about the "perseverance of the saints" can cloud the preacher's interpretation and proclamation of the text. This potential for a biased or hindered understanding of a given biblical text exists for every preacher, from every tradition, including nondenominational or independent churches. A bent toward a particular theological belief is not inevitably detrimental to the preacher, but it is inevitably influential.

The longer I minister and labor alongside brothers and sisters from different theological traditions, the more I am struck by how "we know in part and we prophesy in part" (1 Corinthians 13:9). The awareness that we all see dimly causes me to embrace my own theological tradition with humility. I am a Wesleyan because I believe it is the soundest of all sound doctrines. I'm in this tribe for a reason. And you are in your chosen tribe for a reason. I was educated at a Wesleyan-Holiness university and seminary. But for my doctoral program, I attended an institution of a different theological tradition from my own, and it was one of the best experiences I've ever had. I discovered some amazing people whose doctrine was very different from my own but whose love for Jesus and passion for preaching were the same. It was a humbling experience. We know in part. We prophesy in part.

What does your tradition say about the doctrine of the Holy Spirit? Speaking in tongues? Predestination? Women in ministry? Church polity? Eschatology? We learn about these and other issues in the context of specific faith communities within distinct theological traditions. In some cases, we chose the tradition, and in other cases, the tradition chose us. Whatever our theological heritage, it has inherent strengths, weaknesses, and limitations. To deny this reality is to live in a state of theological infatuation at best, and theological arrogance at worst. The best lenses on earth can't create a perfect understanding of Scripture. We know in part. We prophesy in part.

Location

Much has been written about the importance of understanding Scripture's literary, historical, social, rhetorical, and theological contexts. In order to understand what is happening in the text, we have to understand the context. When was it written? To whom? By whom? For what purpose? Failure to answer these basic questions will certainly lead the preacher to make claims that the text does not make, answer questions the text does not ask, or apply the text to situations it was never meant to address.

Similarly, every preacher has a context too. Over time, our geographical location becomes a lens through which we see the text. Leonora Tubbs Tisdale addresses this topic masterfully in *Preaching as Local Theology and Folk Art*, a book devoted specifically to considering the preacher's context. What are the church's sacred cows and the stories behind them? What is the church's approach to Scripture? What is the church's average level of education? What is the church's average age? What are the church's racial demographics? Reading and interpreting Scripture in a Reformed church in northern Virginia is very different from reading and interpreting Scripture in a Southern Baptist church in Mississippi, or in a Charismatic church in the Midwest. Our location influences what we see or fail to see in the text—and, while context-specific preaching is necessary, we must be aware of the inherent limitations of our location.

When we first arrive in a new place, we are probably more aware of the need to exegete our location: we want to observe it, understand it, identify with it. Like Paul, whose observations about Athens appear in his sermon at Mars Hill, we walk around with our eyes wide open because we know there's a learning curve. Once we've been in a church for a few years, however, it's easier not just to speak the local dialect but also to assume the local mindset. If we are to transcend the limits of our geographical context, we must work hard to stand with one foot in our own context and one foot in the eternal Word of God. Our location can act as a lens that limits our perspective.

I have seen this dynamic in my own life. My first twelve years as a senior pastor were spent in a small town about thirty miles south of Kansas City, Missouri. It was a stable community with one high school and not a lot of racial diversity. Not many new residents moved in, nor did many established residents move out. While there was some poverty, there were no slums, no particularly concentrated clusters of residents lower on the socioeconomic scale. Life in that location affected what I saw in Scripture; it also affected what I missed.

I subsequently moved to Clarksville, Tennessee, one of the fastest-growing cities in the southeastern United States. Seven high schools. Lots of racial diversity. Gang activity. And, most significantly, the second-largest Army installation in the country. As the demographic of the church became increasingly military, I started trying to learn about military culture. It didn't happen overnight—I had no idea what life in the military was like. I didn't know how to read a person's rank by looking at the symbols on the sleeve or the chest. I didn't understand their terminology or the stresses placed on military families dealing with multiple deployments.

In one effort to rectify this, I watched the film series *Band of Brothers* with a group of guys from church, most of whom were active Army or Army veterans. One took charge of the remote and paused the movie every so often to give me lessons: "See the patch on that guy's uniform?

This is where it came from. See how those guys are interacting with each other? This is why."

Over time, living in this context began to impact what I saw in Scripture. For example, in 1 Kings 20:13–27, Ben-Hadad of Samaria attacked Israel. God spoke to Ahab, the king of Israel, through a prophet who assured Ahab that God would bring victory. Ahab of course then asked, "But who will do this?" The message from God was very specific: young officers would lead the way.

One of the things I learned in my *Band of Brothers* crash course was the universal truth that no one knows less about real-world combat than a young officer. Some may be geniuses in the history of warfare, but to gain a real-world education, they have to depend on seasoned NCOs (non-commissioned officers) with common sense and battle experience. Officers lead battles; young officers learn from battles.

Yet God instructed Ahab to choose young officers to lead the fight against Ben-Hadad. Why? God wanted to make it clear that God was the source of Israel's victory. Israel wasn't going to win because they had superior officers; the young officers were going to show that Israel had a superior God. I could have read this text a thousand times in a non-military context and never seen this dynamic.

This context also prompted me to see new meaning in Jesus's words in Luke 17:7–10: "'Suppose one of you has a servant plowing or looking after the sheep. Will he say to the servant when he comes in from the field, "Come along now and sit down to eat"? Won't he rather say, "Prepare my supper, get yourself ready and wait on me while I eat and drink; after that you may eat and drink"? Will he thank the servant because he did what he was told to do? So you also, when you have done everything you were told to do, should say, "We are unworthy servants; we have only done our duty."'"

Before living in a military town, I never realized that Jesus's speech in Luke 17 is the mantra of soldiers who have performed heroic acts on the battlefield. The response I've most often heard to "Thank you for your service" is, "Just doing my job." This answer is straight from Scripture, though I doubt many who use it recognize its origins. Contrast this with church members who get upset if their name is inadvertently left off a recognition or thank-you list. "Just doing my job" causes me to read Luke 17 differently.

Another example occurs in what is often considered the darkest chapter of King David's storied life—his sins of adultery and murder. In 2 Samuel 11, David stayed home while everyone else went to war during the fighting season. Then, according to the NIV, "One evening David got up from his bed and walked around on the roof of the palace" (v. 2). The NRSV says, "One afternoon, when David rose from his couch . . . " as if the king had been taking a nap, or attempting to. Here's how this line opened up the story for me in a new way that would not have happened if I had not lived and pastored in a military community.

We know that David was a seasoned combat veteran. He deployed every spring for years. His accomplishments on the battlefield are well documented. Yet this time, he stayed home. He got up, whether from his bed at night or his couch in the afternoon. Guess what is one of the most common symptoms of post-traumatic stress? Insomnia. Soldiers, ancient and modern, have had trouble sleeping after experiencing war.

This little detail in 2 Samuel 11:2 jumped off the page for the first time when I was preparing to speak to a group of soldiers and their spouses. I had preached from this text before, but previously I hadn't known much at all about PTSD or the ways it affected people. The "aha" from 2 Samuel 11 was a huge one for me. I contend that it happened not just *for* my context but also *because* of my context. The Holy Spirit brought the insight, but that insight was informed by my surroundings.

We all have lenses and limitations, one of which is a specific location. Sometimes it can prevent us from seeing what's in the text. Other times the lens can help us see the text in a way we never would if we were living in a different time or place.

Limited Understanding

Throughout this discussion of lenses I have frequently referred to Paul's words in 1 Corinthians 13: "For we know in part and we prophesy in part, but when the perfect comes, the partial will pass away. Now I know in part; then I shall know fully, even as I have been fully known" (vv. 9–10, 12, ESV). We know what we know, but our knowledge is limited. This is true even after we have done our homework, prayed, heard from God, and know what we are supposed to preach; we never get to the point where we know *everything* about a text. This shouldn't undermine our confidence in what we proclaim; rather, it should temper our confidence with humility. There are few things more off-putting than arrogance or pomposity in the pulpit. It may be difficult to draw the line between confidence and arrogance, but I think we can usually tell when it has been crossed.

Throughout this process of making ourselves ready to preach, we seek the confidence that comes with hearing God's voice, and the humility to know that God didn't tell us everything he knows. Our limitations are real. They should not cause despair or a muffled voice, but they should keep us humble.

PART 2: WHAT TO SAY

■ ■ ■
Sample Sermon: Shameless
Preached by Albert Hung

Albert Hung is the superintendent of the Northern California District for the Church of the Nazarene. He hasn't always lived in the U.S. His time in Taiwan enabled him to gain some insights from Genesis that he might not otherwise have seen.

Genesis 3, Luke 15:11–31, Hebrews 12:2, 1 Peter 2:9–10

Hiding in Plain Sight

Close your eyes. I want you to go somewhere in your mind for a moment. I will warn you ahead of time that this will not be comfortable for some of you. But I want you to trust me. I care about you. Even those of you I'm meeting for the first time today—you especially. I care. We care. We're going to start from a place of personal pain today, but we will end up in a good place, a safe place, a better place. Trust me. Close your eyes.

I'm going to say three little words. Just three. But they wield enormous power.

Listen: "Shame on you." Whose face do you see? Where are you? What's happening? How old are you? How do you feel?

Three little words. Enormous power.

I've noticed something during my years as a pastor. The kinds of people who gravitate toward church are not usually people who think they have it all together. The people who are drawn here have questions. They have a few flaws. Maybe a lot of flaws. The kinds of people who show up here know that they are, in some way, broken. Incomplete. They're looking for something. Sometimes they're running *from* something. If I've just described you, if you're one of those people who feels broken in some way, if you came in carrying a burden of some kind, if you came in with a million questions: I want you to know that you are welcome here. Acknowledging that you're broken doesn't mean you are weak. It makes you honest. And I like honest people. You are my kind of people.

But here's the other thing I've noticed. There's a difference between being honest with ourselves and being honest with each other. What I've noticed over the years is that many of us have trouble being vulnerable.

On every street, in every community, and in every church, there are couples whose marriages are hanging by a thread. Yet nobody knows. There are people who are nearing the end of their lives, and they are scared. Yet nobody knows. There are teens and adults who struggle with same-sex attraction and gender identity. Yet nobody knows. There are families who don't have enough money to last until the end of the month. Yet nobody knows. There are men who are trapped in porn addiction. Women who are having an affair. Nobody knows. There are people who have quietly stopped hoping for things to get better, who have stopped believing in themselves, stopped believing in humanity, stopped believing in God. And nobody knows.

Why do we have such a hard time being vulnerable with each other? What are we afraid of? We come to church because we are looking for hope. We want to be heard, understood, loved, healed. But something holds us back.

It's crazy, isn't it? The church is supposed to be the place where you receive love and support. But we have trouble asking for it.

So here's what I want you to do: turn to the person next to you, and for the next five minutes, I want you to share your deepest, darkest secrets with each other. Go ahead, spill your guts.

I'm kidding! Admit it, you were nervous for a second there.

Some of you are carrying a secret—something very few people know. Perhaps something nobody knows. And it's killing you inside. Or maybe it's not you, but someone close to you. Something is weighing on their heart, and you want to help. But they won't let you in.

Here are the questions we're going to talk about today: What lies behind this impulse to hide from one another? How do we find the courage to come out of hiding so we can get the love and support we need and experience healing? As a church and as a community of faith, is there anything we can do to become a safer place for hurting people?

Crowned with Glory and Honor

The Bible is not a collection of disconnected stories, each of which has a little moral about how to live life. The Bible is a single story. It tells us what's wrong with the human race, what God is going to do about it, and how it all turns out in the end—where history is going. Whenever we recognize we are broken in some way, we can look to Scripture to understand why we are the way we are and how God plans to make things right.

In our last sermon series, we looked at the creation story in the book of Genesis. We look at this passage often because it explains so much about God's original vision for humanity and how it all fell apart. So we're going to visit it again from a slightly different angle.

Genesis 2:7 and 15 say, "The Lord God formed a man from the dust of the ground and breathed into his nostrils the breath of life, and the man became a living being. The Lord God took the man and put him in the Garden of Eden to work it and take care of it."

Human beings are special to God. When God created the heavens, he spoke them into existence. He said, "Let there be light," and *bam*! There was light. But God did not say, "Let there be people," and *bam*, there were people. No. He formed us from the dust, with great tenderness, love, and care. God got his hands dirty when he made you, and he *liked* it. He breathed the breath of life into our nostrils.

Not only that, God has big plans for us. He gives us great honor by putting us in charge of his creation. He wants us to be fruitful and multiply, to fill the earth, subdue it, and rule over it.

This is why King David says in Psalm 8:4–5 (NLT): "What are mere mortals that you should think about them, human beings that you should care for them? Yet you made them only a little lower than God and crowned them with glory and honor."

The Christian understanding of God is that God delights in us. We give him pleasure. We make him happy. God is awfully, awfully fond of you.

In Genesis 2:16–17, the Lord puts the man in the garden to work it and says, "You are free to eat from any tree in the garden; but you must not eat from the tree of the knowledge of good and evil, for when you eat from it you will certainly die."

The Bible portrays God as a wise and loving Father. Wise and loving fathers set boundaries for their children for their own good—and that is what we see here.

What is the boundary? Don't eat from the tree of the knowledge of good and evil—if you do, you will die. Here, the word translated as "knowledge" means "to have mastery over." To eat from the tree of knowledge is to challenge God's authority and to take for ourselves the right to determine what is good and what is evil. God is saying, "That right and responsibility belong to me, and me alone. This is my house. You must abide by my rules. It would not be good for you, my children, with your limited knowledge and experience, to have to determine what is good and what is evil every single day. You are not meant to carry this burden. It would break you. It would be the death of you."

Human beings are given glory and honor above all other living creatures. We are made a little lower than God, but we are not God.

They Felt No Shame

In Genesis 2:18, God said, "It is not good for the man to be alone. I will make him a helper"—a friend, a partner, someone who will watch his back, who will cover his weaknesses, who will lend him strength. And he will do the same for her. And so God creates woman. Human beings are wired for deep, intimate, soul-satisfying relationship, so we see pure joy in the man's response to God's gift in Genesis 2:23: "This is now bone of my bones and flesh of my flesh." The story concludes in verse 25 with the statement, "Adam and his wife were both naked, and they felt no shame."

What a curious little phrase. Why does the story end with these words? Why did the writer feel it was important to say that the man and the woman were naked? And why does he point out that they felt no shame? We might have expected some different commentary, such as, "The man and woman were naked, and they didn't feel cold." Or, " . . . and they were both really muscular."

This statement about shame must be important—really important. Critically important. We have almost no details about what human life was like before the fall—just one chapter in Scripture. But this detail is important enough to be included. It's the last thing we read before it all goes downhill. It's like a summary statement; if we could sum up in just once sentence what life was like before the fall, this would be it: "The man and woman were naked. And they felt no shame."

What Is Shame?

Anthropologists have observed that the cultures of the world tend to fall into one of two categories: guilt-based cultures and shame-based cultures. There is actually a third category known as fear-based cultures, but we'll limit our discussion to the first two.

The United States is a guilt-based culture. But the majority of the world is comprised of shame-based cultures: Asia, Latin America, Africa, the Middle East. What's the difference? Guilt-based cultures are primarily concerned with the individual, with personal responsibility. Shame-based cultures are primarily concerned with the community, with social expectations and obligations.

Think of it this way. Guilt lives in the courtroom. You break a law, you stand alone before a judge, and the judge says, "You are found guilty of wrongdoing and are legally accountable." You are wrong. You have sinned. You expect punishment. You need forgiveness. It's a legal issue.

Shame, however, lives in the community. In other words, what matters most is not what I've done, but what other people think. Shame says, "You don't belong. You are unacceptable, unclean, disgraced." You experience worthlessness and rejection. You need more than forgiveness; you need restoration. You need cleansing, fellowship, love, and acceptance. It's a relational issue.

Guilt is far simpler to understand and remedy than shame. If you are guilty, you pay the penalty, and it's over. Problem solved. Shame, however, is much harder to remove because shame is not about what you've done—it's about who you are. It attacks the very core of your identity and self-worth. Guilt says, "I made a mistake." Shame says, "I *am* a mistake." Shame says, "I am inferior, weak, powerless. A disappointment, a failure. Inadequate, humiliated, filthy. Unlovable, repulsive, disgraced, worthless." The core existential problem for the majority of the world's population is not guilt—it's shame.

And so we cannot overstate the significance of this phrase. It's a profound statement. What is it like to be naked—to be fully exposed, fully known—and feel no shame? To feel completely accepted and secure, with nothing to hide?

God intended for us to live in a world without shame, where we would never feel like we are a disappointment or a mistake, where we would never know what it's like to feel humiliated, alienated, disgraced, worthless, or unlovable. God never wanted us to feel the need to hide.

He created us to be naked before him and each other—fully known, fully accepted, fully loved—without shame. This is paradise. This is what we were created to be.

Naked and Afraid

Now the serpent was more crafty than any of the wild animals the Lord God had made. He said to the woman, "Did God really say, 'You must not eat from any tree in the garden'?"

The woman said to the serpent, "We may eat fruit from the trees in the garden, but God did say, 'You must not eat fruit from the tree that is in the middle of the garden, and you must not touch it, or you will die.'"

"You will not certainly die," the serpent said to the woman. "For God knows that when you eat from it your eyes will be opened, and you will be like God, knowing good and evil."

When the woman saw that the fruit of the tree was good for food and pleasing to the eye, and also desirable for gaining wisdom, she took some and ate it. She also gave some to her husband, who was with her, and he ate it. Then the eyes of both of them were opened, and they realized they were naked; so they sewed fig leaves together and made coverings for themselves.

Then the man and his wife heard the sound of the Lord God as he was walking in the garden in the cool of the day, and they hid from the Lord God among the trees of the garden. But the Lord God called to the man, "Where are you?"

He answered, "I heard you in the garden, and I was afraid because I was naked; so I hid" (Genesis 3:1–10).

For the first time, Adam and Eve had something to hide. They experienced shame and fear. They felt exposed, dirty. And their shame drove a wedge not only between them and God but also between the two of them.

Sin is not simply about breaking a rule. It is a betrayal of a relationship. Sin is not primarily a legal problem—it is a relational problem. Sin is, at its root, a failure to honor God. It is a betrayal of the worst kind: A slap in the face. A punch in the gut. A stab in the back. That is the essence of sin.

Think about it. God created human beings to be special—his crowning achievement, his treasured possession. He created them with tenderness and care, got his hands dirty, bent over them and gave them the breath of life. He gave them an exalted position above all other creatures. He created the woman to be the man's companion and partner. He walked with them in the garden. He loved them. He gave them everything.

And in return, humans said, "That's not enough. You must be holding something back from us. And we want it. We want this knowledge, this mastery over good and evil. We want to be like you. We want to be gods too." With that, they broke the one rule they had been given—and, in doing so, broke their Father's heart. What could be more despicable, more dishonorable, than betraying your own father?

What is the story of the fall of humanity all about? It is the story of how human beings went from having no shame to having no honor. What people in biblical times and in the majority of cultures throughout history have feared most is not guilt, or even death. It's shame.

In Western Christianity, we often say we have a sin problem. We use legal language to portray salvation as a big courtroom scene. God is a just judge; we are guilty of violating the law. Jesus paid the penalty, satisfying God's justice. We are forgiven of our transgressions and reckoned innocent; our sins have been atoned for. And all of this is true—but it is clearly a guilt-based understanding of the gospel. And it's not the whole story.

You see, we don't just have a sin problem—we have a shame problem. Shame poisons our relationships, steals our joy, and drives us into hiding. This is why we have trouble opening up to each other—we are afraid to be fully known. We are afraid of the rejection, the humiliation. We feel dirty, repulsive, unlovable. We are naked, and we know it.

Let me ask you: When did you first realize you were naked? How have you tried to cover up your shame? In what ways do you hide from God and from others?

We have a shame problem. What does the Bible have to say about that?

The Cross: Jesus Bears Our Shame

This is where the good news of Jesus Christ comes in. You see, the gospel tells us that God so loved the world that he sent Jesus Christ not only to bear our sins but also to bear our shame.

When we speak of the cross, we often imagine the physical suffering Jesus endured. You may have heard sermons describing the brutality of crucifixion, right down to a full medical description of the horrific trauma it inflicts on the body. But the biblical writers didn't seem as concerned with Jesus's physical suffering as with the utter humiliation he publicly endured on our behalf. In other words, they describe his shame. Isaiah 53:3–5: "He was *despised* and *rejected* by mankind, a man of suffering, and familiar with pain. *Like one from whom people hide their faces he was despised, and we held him in low esteem.* Surely he took up our pain and bore our suffering, yet we considered him *punished by God, stricken by him, and afflicted*" (emphasis added). This is the language of shame.

Still not convinced? Hebrews 12:1–2 (NLT) makes it crystal clear: "Let us run with endurance the race God has set before us . . . keeping our eyes on Jesus, the champion who initiates and perfects our faith. Because of the joy awaiting him, he endured the cross, disregarding its shame [not its pain—but its shame]. Now he is seated in the place of honor beside God's throne."

Jesus not only bore our sins, but he also bore our shame. The Son of God, on a rescue mission of love, was betrayed, mocked, spit on, stripped, abandoned, and crucified.

Can you see it? Can you see our Savior on the cross? The shame he endured for you, for me, for all of us?

But awareness is not enough to make us whole again. Knowing that Jesus was publicly humiliated on our behalf only adds to our sense of shame. We need something more. We need tangible proof that we are truly forgiven and welcomed back into God's family.

God Restores Our Honor

Jesus gives us the proof we need. In Luke 15:11–24, he tells a parable that helps us understand our heavenly Father's unconditional love on a whole new level. Jesus begins in verse 11: "There was a man who had two sons. The younger one said to his father, 'Father, give me my share of the estate.'"

What the younger son is saying is, "Father, I want your money. I want your land. But I don't want you." Sound familiar? This is the language of betrayal; the language of sin. But the father loves his son, so with a heavy heart, he divides his property and gives the younger son his share. The younger son takes off, travels the world, and squanders his wealth on wild living. Just as he runs out of money, a severe famine strikes the land. He ends up working in a pigpen, up to his knees in excrement. He's hungry, alone, and afraid. He's not even allowed to eat slops from the pig trough.

The shame is unbearable. But he has nowhere to go. So he throws away what's left of his dignity and crawls back home. What can he possibly do or say to make up for dishonoring his father? All he can think to say is, "Father, I have sinned against heaven and against you. I am no longer worthy to be called your son; make me like one of your hired servants" (vv. 18–19). So that's what he plans to do.

What happens next is shocking: "But while [the son] was still a long way off, his father saw him and was filled with compassion for him; he ran to his son, threw his arms around him and kissed him" (v. 20).

Why does the father do this? Why would he run down the road, robes flapping around his ankles, looking like an absolute fool in full view of all his servants? *To spare his son the shame* of walking down the long, dusty road in tattered clothes that smell of pig excrement. To spare him the judging eyes and the murmuring voices. The father humiliates himself as he runs like a fool toward his son, throws his arms around him, buries his nose in his matted hair, and kisses his soiled, dung-covered cheek.

The son does as he planned. He confesses, "Father, I have sinned against heaven and against you. I am no longer worthy to be called your son" (v. 21).

But the father cuts him off and tells his servants, "'Quick! Bring the best robe and put it on him. Put a ring on his finger and sandals on his feet. Bring the fattened calf and kill it. Let's have a feast and celebrate. For this son of mine was dead and is alive again; he was lost and is found.' So they began to celebrate" (vv. 22–24).

What is the father doing? He is restoring his son by lavishing honor upon him. More importantly, he honors him in public, in plain view of everyone. He wants there to be no doubt: "My son is home. He is forgiven. He is accepted. My son, my son, my son is home!"

The Power of Honor

The gospel does not end with Jesus paying for our sins. Nor does it end with him bearing our shame. The gospel, the good news of Jesus Christ, tells us that Jesus clothes us with dignity, restores our honor, crowns us with glory, and invites us to reign with him in the kingdom of heaven. He has given us fine white robes to wear. We are cloaked in Jesus's righteousness.

He has given us a seal, a symbol of his power and authority, the Holy Spirit. He has thrown us a party, invited us to sit at his banquet table, signifying that we are welcomed unconditionally back into God's family. He has exalted us to a position of great honor and privilege and has given us purpose, something to live and die for.

Whoever believes in Christ will never be put to shame. First Peter 2:9–10 tells us, "You are a chosen people, a royal priesthood, a holy nation, God's special possession . . . Once you were not a people, but now you are the people of God."

God has honored you; the gospel is the story of how he did it. The God of the universe came down in the flesh to *serve you*—Jesus became your servant. Jesus discloses God's true feelings toward us.

We say to God: "Lord, I have sinned against heaven and against you. I am no longer worthy to be called your child."

And God responds: "My child, my child, I love you. I sent my one and only, perfect son to bear your shame, clothe you with dignity, and restore your honor. You are accepted. So that you believe it, and so that everyone else believes it, you will receive honor, worth, and even glory, and *it will be public.*"

Does that sound like good news to you? It does to me.

How does this make you feel toward God? Doesn't it make you want to cry tears of happiness? Doesn't it make you want to leap for joy? Doesn't it make your heart burst with love?

Your shame has been lifted. You are accepted by God. You will receive honor, worth, and even glory, and it will be public.

Come out of hiding. Come home. Let Jesus lead you into his Father's house—*our* Father's house. Come home.

A Final Word: How Then Should Our Church Respond?

Is there anything we can do to help the church become a safer place for people to be vulnerable? Absolutely. Because shame is relational, it must be healed in community. Shame begins in the community and must be healed in community.

First, we must be a church that refuses to heap more shame on already shame-filled people.

Second, we must become a church where people are unconditionally accepted and radically honored. We must demonstrate in tangible ways that broken and shame-filled people will receive a full and enthusiastic welcome here. They will be lavished with grace and love. And in the weeks to come, we will talk about how we accomplish that.

Brené Brown writes in *Daring Greatly*, "Shame derives its power from being unspeakable. If we can share our story with someone who responds with empathy and understanding, shame can't survive."[7]

It's not enough that people are forgiven of their sins. They must also be publicly welcomed into the community, into the family of God.

Your shame has been lifted. You are accepted by God. You will receive honor, worth, and even glory, and it will be public.

Closing Exercise

Close your eyes. Go back to the scene I asked you to imagine at the beginning of the sermon. Where are you? Whom do you see?

Again, you hear the words, "Shame on you." But you see something you didn't before—some*one* you didn't see before. You see Jesus walking toward you. He steps between you and your accuser, puts his hands on your shoulders, and looks you in the eyes. He is smiling. Gentle. Kind.

Without taking his eyes off of you, he calls out, "Quick! Bring out the best robe." You feel something soft and heavy drape over your shoulders. You look down, and you are dressed in the finest white robe. The same one Jesus is wearing.

You hear singing—hundreds of voices singing. They're shouting, "Holy! Holy! Holy is the Lord God Almighty! The whole earth is full of his glory! Worthy is the Lamb who has been slain and sits at the right hand of God!"

You look around for your accusers, but they are nowhere to be seen.

Jesus says, "My friend, you are welcome here. Come sit at our Father's table."

He puts his arm around your shoulder and leads you to a banquet table laden with choice foods of every kind. This table seems to have no end; there are people as far as the eye can see. Jesus leads you to an empty seat and pulls the chair out for you. You sit, and everyone starts applauding. Cheering. You are home.

---

7. Brené Brown, *Daring Greatly: How the Courage to Be Vulnerable Transforms the Way We Live, Love, Parent, and Lead* (New York: Avery, an imprint of Penguin Random House, 2012).

five ▪ TOOLS FOR ENGAGING THE TEXT: ASKING THE RIGHT QUESTIONS

■ I'M NOT a fan of a steady diet of topical preaching. The starting point for topical preaching, instead of the Bible, is an issue of interest that has been identified by the preacher or congregation. Examples include topics like marriage, divorce, finances, friendship, parenting, sexuality, poverty, war, abortion, or the legalization of marijuana. In earlier eras, topical preaching addressed issues like slavery, prohibition, and civil rights. These topics are of interest to hearers who would like to know what God says about a given subject. We find some of this in Scripture itself when Paul writes portions of his letters to address specific questions previously asked by congregations in places like Corinth or Rome about how to relate to governmental authority or handle relational rifts in the church.

While preaching can and should relate to real-world issues, I advocate an approach to preparation that is thoroughly driven by the biblical text. Beginning with a topic instead of beginning with Scripture can lead to hearers perceiving the Bible as a book that exists primarily to provide answers to their questions, rather than one that helps us see what questions we should be asking to begin with. Topical preaching can turn Scripture into a divine how-to or self-help book that we master instead of a means through which we learn what it means to be mastered by the God who gave us the Word. All preaching should be relevant, and there are certainly times when a topical sermon can be the best approach, but I contend that the best starting point for a sermon is Scripture.

If the end goal of preparation is hearing what to preach and how to preach it, then preparation begins with listening—not just to the musings and questions of our congregations and ourselves but also to the text and to the God of the text. So how do we go about listening to the text?

We converse with the text by asking a lot of questions. In the following pages, you will see a variety of questions. You may want to incorporate some of them into your weekly preparation process—these are tool-belt questions, the ones you'll use regularly. There will be other questions you may want to save for later—these are toolbox questions. The tools in the box aren't used on every job; they are specialized tools for specific projects. You bring them out when they're useful for the job at hand.

Toolbox questions are important because we need to have more at our disposal than the tried-and-true methods we use every week; sometimes a less-familiar-but-still-effective tool is needed. You will likely find that the lists and discussions that follow contain more tools than you can fit on your belt; if so, consider making room for them in your box.

The Importance of Asking Questions

Thomas H. Troeger writes, "Basic questions help us get behind the text to imagine the details not written but implied. These are the 'who, where, what, why, and when' questions, the 'see, hear, smell, taste, and touch' questions, and the questions that identify our own emotional and intellectual response to the text."[1]

Thomas G. Long says,

The art of biblical exegesis, put very simply, involves learning how to ask questions of a biblical text. Two major problems can cause this to go awry: We can ask the wrong questions, and we can refuse to listen to the responses that the text gives to good questions. When we only ask the questions to which we believe we already possess the answers, we have asked the wrong questions. When we resist being surprised or troubled by the text, we have shut our ears to its voice.[2]

---

1. Thomas H. Troeger, *Imagining a Sermon* (Nashville: Abingdon Press, 1990), 64.
2. Thomas G. Long, *The Witness of Preaching* (Louisville: Westminster John Knox Press, 1989), 66.

When it comes to asking questions, some preachers have a systematic approach; others have a much more fluid process. We can range anywhere from the single question, "What am I supposed to preach from this text?" to a series of questions that have the potential to yield sermonic possibilities. Below are some sample questions formulated by David Busic (general superintendent for the Church of the Nazarene) and Jeren Rowell (president of Nazarene Theological Seminary) and offered to pastors at various training events. This list can be helpful, both to new preachers looking to develop a systematic approach and to seasoned preachers looking for fresh ways to engage Scripture:

1. What kind of text is this?
2. What is the text trying to do?
3. What kind of community is this text addressing?
4. Here is the trouble in this text:
5. Where is the gospel in this text?
6. What should I do about this text?
7. How does the text "sound"?
8. What are the congregational blocks to this text? [In other words, what will the congregation have a hard time hearing or accepting about this text? How might the congregation's context and collective biases stand in the way of their hearing?]
9. What is this text doing to me, the preacher?
10. What other texts speak to this one—or against this one?
11. What points of view are present in this text?
12. What does this text *not* answer or say?
13. How do I exegete the congregation in light of this text? [Just as each biblical text has a specific context, every sermon is preached in a specific context. Knowledge of both will help us shape sermons that are true to the biblical text *and* fitting for our unique congregational context.[3]]
14. What is the one idea I want people to take away from this text?

---

3. Leonora Tubbs Tisdale's *Preaching as Local Theology and Folk Art* equips preachers for the work of congregational exegesis.

I will share a few more lists from other sources before moving to a discussion of the questions that form my own practice of preparation. This list of questions comes from Thomas G. Long:

1. Write a paraphrase of the text.
2. If the text is a narrative, stand in the shoes of each of the characters and experience the story from these varied perspectives.
3. Explore the text looking for details that appear, at first glance, to be unusual or out of place.
4. Ask if the text has a center of gravity: that is, a main thought around which all other thoughts are organized.
5. Look for conflict, either in the text or behind it.
6. Look for connections between the text and what comes before and after it.
7. View the text through many different "eyes." How would this passage appear to a man? A woman? A child? A rich person? A poor person? A homosexual person? An unemployed person? A parent? A Jew?
8. Think of the text, as J Randall Nichols suggests, "as someone's attempt to reflect on the answer to some important question," and then try to discern what the question could be.
9. Ask, as Craddock suggests, what the text is *doing*. Is it commanding, singing, narrating, explaining, warning, debating, praying, reciting?[4]

I got this last list of questions from a colleague of mine, Judy Rois of the ACTS (Association of Chicago Theological Schools) doctorate of ministry program; she acquired it from Eduard R. Riegert, a professor at Martin Luther University College (formerly Waterloo Lutheran Seminary):

1. Establish the limits of the pericope.
2. Do a "plot analysis" of the text.
   a. If the text is a story, identify:
      i. Setting
      ii. Complications

---

4. Long, *The Witness of Preaching*, 68–72.

         iii. Climax
         iv. Resolution
     b. If the text is not a story, identify its movements. [Where does it change in tone or subject? What about other transitions in thought, style, or intensity? Every text will have some kind of movement within or underneath it. Where and how is it moving?]
3. Identify where you enter the text. Where does it:
    a. grab me?   b. engage me?
    c. challenge me?   d. confuse me?
    e. threaten me?   f. convict me?
    g. inspire me?   h. appeal to me?
    i. intrigue me?   j. tease me?
    k. anger me?   l. surprise me?
    m. enlighten me?   n. liberate me?
    o. comfort me?   p. shove, push, prod, or trip me?
4. What does the text say? Do a homiletical exegesis:
    a. Contexts: historical, editorial, scriptural
    b. Form: narrative, poetry, law, prophecy, wisdom, Gospel, epistle, apocalyptic, parable, miracle?
    c. Important words: Conduct a verse-by-verse examination and exposition; read more than one translation; look at the original language; use a commentary and lexicon.
    d. Theological concerns: how would you connect this text with the tradition of Christian theological thinking?
    e. Analogies of experience: what parallels to our experiences and circumstances does the text suggest?
    f. Creative brooding: allow the text to interact with life (note: this has already begun in #3)
         i. Ask: What sort of world is exposed, suggested, posited, or revealed by the text?
         ii. Ask: What new world does the text reveal?
         iii. Ask: How do we respond to the invitation to enter this new world?

g. Obstacles to communication: linguistic, historical, theological, existential
h. Purpose of the sermon—define this as distinctly as possible:
    i. Proclamation: proclaim what, to whom, why?
    ii. Teaching: teach what, to whom, why?
    iii. Healing: heal what, in whom, why?
    iv. Always ask, "So what?"

I have my own list as well. In the chapters that follow, I'll share the questions I typically ask about every text from which I preach. These are by no means the only questions you could or should ask; they are simply intended to help me listen to the text and to the God of the text. I have found that the first "aha" moment can come anywhere in my homiletic process. Sometimes the issue of what to say is resolved with the first question I ask. Sometimes it emerges with the third, fourth, or fifth. Other times, it doesn't emerge until I've puzzled long and hard over what to ask next. The questions I share in the following chapters are ones I have found to be helpful in engaging the text and attempting to hear it on its own terms.

six ▪ TOOLS FOR ENGAGING THE TEXT: INITIAL OBSERVATIONS

▪ **ASSUMING** the text has already been selected, the first step in the homiletic process is to sit down with the text and a blank screen (or, if you prefer, a blank pad of paper). Think of yourself as an explorer, a sleuth, the recipient of a letter from a friend or lover—whatever enables you to intently engage the text. Have a conversation with the text. Ask questions. Make observations. Argue. Reflect. Reminisce.

Each preacher must figure out her or his own process for preparation, but I try to allow a lot of time for the text to do its work on and in me before I share my thoughts with the congregation. So I start my preparation process not just a few days before but typically three to four *weeks* before I preach a text. I don't want to feel pressured to find something to say. I want to be relaxed, open, and patient with the Word. The goal is not (yet) to develop a sermon but to listen, observe, question, remember, and simply be *in* the text, in order to become familiar with it. What stands out? What raises questions? What memories are evoked? What words are repeated? What theological statements need to be explored? I call this phase "initial observations." Others call it "free association." Whatever you call it, the purpose of this phase is to spend time in the text and begin to converse with it.

Why begin three to four weeks before preaching from the text? For me, there are several reasons:

1) While there will be other scriptures to study and sermons to write in those three to four weeks, this initial exposure to the text will allow it to germinate, grow, and take root in my life.

2) Other members of the pastoral staff, including the worship pastor, children's pastor, and youth pastor go through this process with me. Eventually we will spend time looking at the text as a group. I don't want someone else's interpretation of the text to short-circuit my personal engagement with it. I want the first voice I hear to be that of the Spirit.

3) The sermon is always preached in a liturgical context. Just as it takes time for the sermon to develop, it takes time to plan other aspects of worship. Allowing everyone involved in planning and leading the service three to four weeks to prepare usually results in a more intentional, more worshipful experience.

4) Spending more time in the text enhances our ability to understand and proclaim it to the congregation. As Jeffrey Arthurs writes: "Preachers who want to re-create the rhetorical impact of the text must *embody* it . . . So if the text is joyful, we are to feel that happiness, then speak out of a full heart with a skillful voice and bearing. If the text is doleful, we need to enter vicariously the . . . experience and then communicate that experience naturally and sincerely. When we embody the text, the rhetorical impact is generated in the hearts and minds of the people."[1]

The first time I read a text, I stop wherever and whenever something hits me; typically, it happens with every verse. I bring my questions, observations, experiences, and memories into the document. I may engage a biblical character in conversation, ask theological questions, or make a list of other scriptures that seem to support or contradict the one at hand. I might note any words I want to research further. If I've preached on the text before, I might write down what I remember from previous exegetical work. If I've heard someone else preach on the text, I'll put down any impressions or quotes I remember from that sermon. If the text brings

---

1. Jeffrey D. Arthurs, *Preaching with Variety: How to Re-Create the Dynamics of Biblical Genres* (Grand Rapids, MI: Kregel Publications, 2007), 59.

to mind a current event, a person, a personal experience, or something I read in a book, I'll note those thoughts too.

Making these initial observations can take anywhere from a few minutes to a few hours, depending on the length of the text and my level of engagement. The key is not to see how fast I can do it but to engage deeply and notice what starts to stir in me. Does the text evoke joy, confusion, gratitude, conviction, guilt? I want to see the movement, discern the plot, imagine the stories and the people behind the text. Usually only a small percentage of what's in these notes ends up in the final sermon, but that's not the point. The goal at this point is not to get a sermonic spark (although that does sometimes happen). I'm trying to avoid pimping the Word. Rather, I want to engage it, and I want God to engage me through it.

There isn't a wrong way to go about this process, as long as it isn't rushed. Not all of our initial observations will be exegetically, historically, or theologically accurate. We might see things that aren't there, or we might miss things that are there; but as we ask other questions, consult the scholars, and reread the text, we will have some of our initial observations corrected and others confirmed.

I am convinced that when we jump too quickly into finding out what others have written about a passage, we miss opportunities to encounter God in and through the text. An unhealthy dependency on other preachers, authors, or scholars can make us lazy or, worse, irresponsible. If it's been a while since you sought to hear from the text first before hearing from another person, you might be surprised by what the Spirit has to show you.

One of the reasons this practice is often neglected goes back to the idea of preachers becoming pimps—we go to the Word to get something we can give to others. With numerous people, projects, and problems clamoring for our time and attention, spending a few hours in a process that may or may not yield sermonic material might seem impractical. We might question whether this is the best use of our time. But if we believe that the call to preach includes the call to prepare ourselves adequately, then this first step can be indispensable. Personally, I have found it to be exactly that. I am confident that if you put this first step into practice, you too will find it to be one of the most intriguing, even exhilarating, parts of your preparation.

Jesus said that the mouth speaks out of the overflow of the heart (see Luke 6:45). As we engage the text in this initial step of preparation, we seek for the Word to take root in our hearts. To me, this is an indispensable part of making myself ready. I hope you'll give it a try.

seven ▪ TOOLS FOR ENGAGING THE TEXT: GENRE

The preacher begins the preparation process by gaining an effective familiarity with the text that will be utilized. Otherwise, form will not follow function.
—Eugene Lowry[1]

■ **GENRE** is a French word that means "category." We deal with genres every day. On restaurant menus, we see different genres of food: appetizers, sandwiches, salads. Entrees may have subgenres of chicken, seafood, or beef. And of course, there's my favorite menu genre—desserts. The menu is organized by genre so the diner need not search for salad dressing flavors between chocolate cake and caramel pie. At clothing stores, signs indicate genres of apparel: men, women, petite, extra tall. Hardware stores like Home Depot and Lowe's are organized by project genre: plumbing, electrical, flooring, lighting. We also find genres in music stores: rock, classic rock, funk, jazz, blues, hip-hop, opera, grunge, screamo, polka . . . you get the idea.

Regarding genre in film, movie critic Roger Ebert wrote, "A movie is not about what it is about. It is about how it is about it."[2] On this, Grant

---

1. Eugene Lowry, *How to Preach a Parable: Designs for Narrative Sermons* (Nashville: Abingdon Press, 1989), 31.

2. Roger Ebert, *Questions for the Movie Answer Man* (Kansas City: Andrews McMeel Publishing, 1997), 270.

Holbrook notes, "Of course the 'what' is important, but a focus on the 'how' can prove helpful in shedding new light."[3]

More to the point for our discussion of preaching, there are genres of literature, including biblical literature. Genre is important because what Ebert says about movies is also true of the biblical text—it's not just what it is about but how it is about it. As literary critic Stanley Fish wrote, "We make interpretive decisions based upon our assumptions about the sort of communication we are receiving, and once those decisions are made, a certain set of operations swings into place."[4] Different genres function in different ways, as we see below:[5]

Genre	**Function**
Once upon a time . . . (fairy tale/fable/myth)	teach a moral lesson
Knock, knock . . . (joke)	delight/entertain
For Sale: 1997 Honda Civic . . . (advertisement)	solicit/inform
Last Will and Testament of . . . (legal document)	bind/bless/curse/bequeath
Roses are red, violets are blue . . . (poetry)	delight/inspire/describe/reflect/observe/condemn
Last summer we went to Daytona Beach, and . . . (narrative/story)	share life/reminisce/entertain

---

3. *Join the Feast;* "Mark 9:30–37," by Grant Holbrook in *Join the Feast,* a blog Lectionary resource from Union-PSCE.

4. Quoted in Thomas G. Long, *Preaching and the Literary Forms of the Bible* (Minneapolis: Fortress Press, 1989), 17.

5. See also Haddon Robinson and Craig Brian Larson, editors, *The Art & Craft of Biblical Preaching: A Comprehensive Resource for Today's Communicators* (Grand Rapids: Christianity Today International, 2005), 229. Other great resources on this topic include Jeffrey D. Arthurs, *Preaching with Variety: How to Re-Create the Dynamics of Biblical Genres* (Grand Rapids: Kregel Publications, 2007); Mike Graves, *The Sermon As Symphony: Preaching the Literary Forms of the New Testament* (Valley Forge, PA: Judson Press, 1997); and Long, *Preaching and the Literary Forms.*

Let me give you some advice . . . (wisdom/proverb)	inform/chastise/help
To Whom It May Concern . . . (formal correspondence)	inform
Dear John . . . (breakup letter)	end a relationship
My dearest darling . . .	delight/share love/build relationship
Step 1: Attach part A to part B . . . (instruction manual)	instruct/guide/teach
I am writing in response to last week's article . . . (editorial)	argue/disagree/convince/affirm
On December 7, 1941 . . . (textbook)	teach/inform

In his *Reflections on the Psalms*, C. S. Lewis wrote, "There is a . . . sense in which the Bible, since it is after all literature, cannot properly be read except as literature; and the different parts of it as the different sorts of literature they are."[6] In the sixty-six books of the Bible, we find historical narrative, law, wisdom, epistle, apocalyptic literature, satire—and this is by no means an exhaustive list, but you get the idea. The Bible is not only what it is about, but how it is about saying it. The genre of a text should inform its interpretation.

Long notes that, just as there are different rules for different sports, there are different rules for different genres: "Catching the ball and running as far as I can with it may be a brilliant play in football but a blunder in baseball. If the speaker is playing one game and the listener another, communication breaks down."[7]

What happens when we attempt to interpret a parable as the law, or a poetic hymn as ethical discourse? It kills the text! Likewise, if we treat

---

6. C. S. Lewis, *Reflections on the Psalms* (Boston: Houghton Mifflin Harcourt, 1958), 3. Quoted in Arthurs, *Preaching with Variety*, 21.

7. Long, *Preaching and the Literary Forms*, 15.

different texts as though they all fit into the same box, we fail to let Scripture speak for itself. We must observe not only what the text says but also how it says it. Why a parable instead of didactic discourse? Why a simile instead of plain speech? It is beneficial to reflect on why the writer chose the particular form at hand. As Darius Salter writes:

> Surprising to most preachers and to far more churchgoers is that God's story is entertaining, enjoyable, intriguing, fascinating, and captivating, as well as paradoxical, dialectical, mystifying, and at times downright bewildering. What we have in Scripture are stories, songs, poems, metaphors, images, letters, and almost innumerable figures of speech that were the polished art of accomplished communicators. God is anything but dull, and His story is anything but dull. God has not simply told us a story; He has told it with the imagination, creativity, and art that characterize His mind."[8]

With that in mind, let's look at a few biblical genres and their function:

Genre	Example Reference	Function
Law/commandment	Exodus 20/Leviticus/Matthew 6:1; 22:37–40	practical instruction
Genealogy	Numbers/Matthew 1	record ancestry
Poetry/music/prayer	Psalms	lament/praise
Wisdom literature (with many subsets of genres within)	Job/Proverbs/Ecclesiastes, etc.	advise/guide/teach/make a point
Prophetic	Isaiah/Jeremiah/Hosea, etc.	predict/prepare/warn
Prayer	John 17/Ephesians 3:14–19	teach/reveal/encourage

---

8. Salter, *Preaching as Art*, 18.

Narrative	Acts	recount or record history/inspire/inform
Theological discourse	Romans	inform/persuade
Epistle	Galatians/Ephesians/Philippians/Colossians, etc.	guide/instruct/shepherd/address specific issues
Apocalyptic	Revelation/Daniel	cast a hopeful vision

It typically doesn't take long to discern the genre of a given text, but spending some time reflecting on why the writer chose to say it like they said it is always going to be beneficial.

I would like to note here that we must consider the form of the text in determining the form of the sermon. Years ago I heard Fred Craddock bemoan preaching that takes lively, image-rich, plot-thick biblical narratives and reduces them to two or three points; he likened it to boiling off the coffee and preaching the stain at the bottom of the cup. Jeffrey Arthurs treats this subject well in *Preaching with Variety,* where he writes: "We use variety because the text does. The form of the sermon should reproduce some impact of the form of the text. You fill a quiver with different kinds of arrows to hit different kinds of targets, not to display your prowess as an archer."[9]

The goal of sermon formation is not creativity for creativity's sake or variety for variety's sake. Rather, sermon formation provides an opportunity for preachers to be as varied in proclamation as the texts from which they preach.

---

9. Arthurs, *Preaching with Variety,* 18.

eight ▪ TOOLS FOR ENGAGING THE TEXT: IMAGE OF GOD

■ **WHO** is God? How do we see God? How does God see us? How does God interact with his creation? What does *this particular text* reveal about the character of God? While the congregation may not be asking these questions every week, we preachers should be. Every text we preach reveals something about the nature and character of God.

Our congregants will form their ideas and images of God from the words we say, the scriptures we share, and the ways we present God. In some cases, we will be building on a healthy understanding of God instilled by godly parents, great teachers, other preachers, and the congregants' own engagement with the Word. In other cases, the people to whom we preach will have a skewed, inaccurate, or unhealthy understanding of God. Part of our role is to help them see God as he reveals himself through the Word.[1]

False conceptions or images of God are common in the church. I'm sure we've all encountered someone whose image of God the Father was based on a bad earthly father. Some people see God as overbearing, condescending, and impossible to please. Others view God as permissive, distant, or uninvolved. I have met well-meaning people who understand God as primarily a lawgiver, and as a result, they themselves are legalistic.

---

1. I am working from the assumption that readers of this book are intentional about preaching from a variety of texts. While we all have our favorite passages and genres, we must be purposeful in providing a well-rounded diet of the biblical witness. We have to move outside our comfort zones in selecting texts from which to preach.

There are also those who have made God in their own image—whether that's passive or aggressive, gentle or harsh, lamb-carrying nurturer or temple-cleansing terror. While we can't guarantee that people won't do the same thing as they hear our sermons, we can be intentional about the image of God we convey.

We can begin to form an image of God in the text by asking questions of the text, such as: What is God doing here? What is God saying? How is God acting or reacting? Does this text present God as Father, Judge, Creator, Redeemer? Is God the Son present, absent, sorrowful, joyful? Is God the Spirit being worshiped, demanding allegiance, mobilizing people? Is God offering grace or announcing judgment? Is God working through people or in spite of them? Is God calming storms or disrupting the status quo? Is God laying down the law or laying down his life? Every text—*every text*—tells us something about the nature and character of God. If we are true to the text—every text, every week—the congregation will develop a healthy image of God.

Our image of God has significant behavioral implications. We've all encountered "Christians" whom we felt grossly misrepresented God. Maybe they were holding signs proclaiming God's hatred, or declaring God's acceptance of any and all human behavior—in both cases, these are distortions that have been formed over time. This goes to show how belief determines behavior; whatever we believe about God will manifest in the way we live. If we believe God is holy, we will live as holy people. If we believe God is loving, we will behave lovingly toward God and toward others. If we believe God is just waiting for us to mess up so we can be judged, we will live in fear or anger.

How does this happen? How do we form our understandings or misunderstandings about God? Certainly by what we read and what we've been taught—but we also form an understanding of God from what we hear preached. As preachers, we must make every effort to ensure that the people to whom we preach understand God the way he presents himself in the Word.

We can practice finding the image of God in the following sample passages:

Psalm 62:5–12

David speaks of finding rest in God alone and calls others to put their trust in God rather than in riches, extortion, or stolen goods. In this text God is trustworthy and provides rest and salvation. He is a mighty rock, a fortress, a refuge. His love is unfailing. He makes judgments and gives rewards with steadfast love; he is powerful, personal, accessible, loving. This psalm provides a deep, beautiful well from which to draw images of God for a sermon.

Mark 12:41–44

Jesus is in the temple with his disciples. As they sit near the offering box, Jesus draws attention to a widow's offering that is both small and sacrificial. Though this selection is only three verses long, it shows us several things about God: he sees what people are doing, understands the motives behind our actions, bases his approval on more than meets the eye, and draws attention to the marginalized.

Acts 4:5–12

Peter responds to the Sanhedrin after their interrogation regarding the healing of the lame beggar (Acts 3). In his response, we see many images of God: God is triune (Father, Son, and Spirit are all mentioned in this passage). God fills us and empowers us. He was crucified and resurrected. He is a healer who works through people like Peter and John. He is the cornerstone, the authority, the deliverer, has a powerful name, and is the only source of salvation.

As Todd Johnson, professor at Fuller Theological Seminary, once said, "The measure of a good sermon is when people leave saying not, 'What a great sermon,' but rather, 'What a great God.'"[2] The image of God that we present is critical.[3]

---

2. Todd Johnson during a class lecture for the ACTS DMin program, June 30, 2005, Chicago.

3. I am not the sole contributor to the textual analyses above; I drew much of the material from documents created for our pastoral staff's weekly study.

PART 2: WHAT TO SAY

■ ■ ■
Sample Sermon:
Overhearing the Regret of God
Preached by Dan Boone

This sermon was the first in a series preached by Dan Boone, president of Trevecca Nazarene University. Dan is a prolific author and incredible preacher. I have quoted from his Preaching the Story that Shapes Us *several times in this book.*

You might note that this sermon violates one of the primary rules of preaching: never end with bad news. But this particular sermon was the first of seven in a series on Noah. Though we're used to framing this narrative in terms of animal pairs and rainbows, it's actually a terrifying story. Boone says, "I wanted to get behind this image and look at the dark side of God that is often overlooked. For this reason, I decided to let the unsettledness of the sermon ending launch us into the series." This is a sermon that was inspired by and built on the image of God in the text.

Genesis 5:28–6:8

It was a whisper spoken in the privacy of their bedroom. The boy who had given them fits had become a man. He had rebelled, disobeyed, disrespected them. And now, with his recent violence, he had broken his parents' hearts. His latest escapade had gone beyond broken rules—he had left broken bodies. His parents were in their bedroom talking. The lights had long been off; sleep was long past due. He was out there somewhere, still doing violence to people. One parent whispered words of anguished regret: "I wish we'd never had him." If the boy had been standing there, had overheard the whispers of his grieved parents, would it have made any difference?

That's the question we are faced with in the story of Noah and the ark. In this well-known, well-loved story, we are brought face-to-face with the regret of God. We overhear God say, "I wish I'd never made them"—and he's talking about you and me.

Our story does not begin with regret. It begins with the words, "God saw that it was good" (Genesis 1). God is pleased with his creation and his creatures. God and the humans stroll the garden and discuss horticulture and animal monikers. They share common interests in work and play. They take the same break at the end of each week. They are partners in creation.

Sample Sermon: Dan Boone

Humans are the epitome of God's handiwork. God has made space in the universe for the existence of will other than his own will. They are free. They are empowered to cooperate with God in the management of the world. It is good—very good.

But in Genesis 3, things begin to unravel in a terrible way. Eve sees something she wants and seizes it. Adam follows suit. No longer satisfied with their partnership with God, they wish to be self-sustaining, independent creatures. They will fend for themselves now that they know good and evil. They run and hide, and in hiding, they discover their desire to cover themselves before God and before each other. It is no longer safe to be naked in the world.

Curses follow: Eve bears babies in pain; Adam farms fields in sweat; the ground grows weeds. They're a long way from the idyllic garden-tending arrangement they began with. And the worst is yet to come: Eve gives painful birth to two boys, one of whom eventually murders the other. More babies are born, and evil multiplies exponentially across the earth. God's vision of a good creation is going downhill faster than a Disney roller coaster.

Genesis 6 begins with one of the weirdest stories in the whole Bible. The sons of God look down on the daughters of humans and are captivated by their beauty. They see what they want and seize it, just like Eve did with the forbidden fruit (it's the same Hebrew word). The result of their offspring is a race of warriors, people skilled at killing each other. Cain's murderous art has been perfected by this marriage between the sons of God and the daughters of humans. And with eternal blood in them, there will be no end to the murderous deeds of humankind. At this point in the story, God limits human life to 120 years; God caps evil.

The next words in the story may well be some of the most sobering in all of Scripture: "The Lord saw that the wickedness of humankind was great in the earth, and that every inclination of the thoughts of their hearts was only evil continually. And the Lord was sorry that he had made humankind on the earth, and it grieved him to his heart. So the Lord said, "I will blot out from the earth the human beings I have created—people together with animals and creeping things and birds of the air, for I am sorry that I have made them" (Genesis 6:5–7 NRSV).

We're on page 5 of a 1,009-page story called the Bible, and the main character is having second thoughts. In five pages we've gone from "God saw that it was good" to "God saw and regretted." The word used to describe the grief in God's heart is the same word used for the pain in the woman's womb—the curse has gotten into God. God's creatures are seeing and seizing, and they are destroying the earth. Violence (*hamas* in Hebrew) covers the earth. Humans cannot transcend their self-interest to care for one another.

I've always thought of the story of Noah and the ark as a good story about animal pairs and rainbows in the sky—not anymore. It is the story of God's regret. It is the story of a dark moment when God decides to act on his regret and wash us all away.

God-talk interests me. My friends often speak of God in mechanical, pre-planned ways. They recount these opening chapters of our story like this: Before God made Adam and Eve, he already knew they were going to make a royal mess of things, but he went ahead and made them anyway. After they misbehaved, he slapped a few curses on them to let them know they couldn't get away with such behavior. Then he kicked them out of the garden to give them a taste of the world on their own. Things got worse, but God wasn't worried. He just sent a catastrophic flood to get everyone's attention. Then he preserved the memory of the flood in an ark. Noah made sure everyone who came after the flood knew about the time God got sick and tired of humans messing up his world.

That's how I hear people tell this part of the story—mechanical. No surprises. God arranged it all beforehand. God lined up the dominoes and let them fall. But I have trouble with that way of telling the story.

This past Christmas, my family got hooked on dominoes, and we learned a domino game called Mexican Train. You pile the dominoes in the middle of the table and each player takes 15. To start the game, you place the double-twelve in the middle of the table. Each player then starts his or her own train off the double-twelve. The strategy is to line up your dominoes in numeric order, connecting them in one straight line. You alone can play on your train. You hope to play each domino in order—but there are ways to mess people up. You can play a double on your train and leave it open, which means the next person has to cover your open double before he or she can play anywhere else. People start groaning when a player pulls one domino from the middle of perfectly arranged dominoes waiting to be played; now there is a gap in the numerical sequence. Your train has been derailed by a rogue double—your competitor has messed up your train.

As I read Genesis 6, I see that God hadn't counted on the mess we made. It wasn't pre-planned. God wasn't tipping dominoes by himself—God was playing with partners. And when we played rogue dominoes on our train, God had to respond. This isn't how God intended the game to go. As I read the text, I see that, had God known in Genesis 1:1 what he knew in Genesis 6:5, he never would have emptied the box onto the table. Like the parents whispering in the bedroom, he wished we'd never been born.

Denise and I have enjoyed watching our daughters act in dramatic performances. I remember when Abby was in a high school production of *Arsenic and Old Lace*. I'd seen the play before, so I knew the plotline; I wouldn't be holding my breath to see how it turned out. But if I were reading the Bible for the first time and came to this story on page five of Holy Scripture, I'd be thinking some serious thoughts about the characters. These humans really are free to wreak destruction . . . and so is God. Only God is a lot better at blotting things out.

The freedom of God is more frightening than the freedom of humans. God is on the verge of giving up his vision for a partnership. God is deeply grieved and regrets having ever made us—he is deciding to pull the plug on the universe. God is vulnerable to the evil we do—it gets to him. God can be pushed too far. Did you know that?

nine ▪ TOOLS FOR ENGAGING THE TEXT: UNIVERSALS IN HUMAN EXPERIENCE

■ **NOT** everyone has been on a fishing boat in the Sea of Galilee, but we've all been in a storm. Not everyone has stared back at a crowd full of scowling people waiting to throw stones, but we've all felt condemnation. Not everyone has encountered a nine-foot-tall giant, but we've all faced challenges that were bigger than ourselves. Not everyone has seen a married couple struck dead because they lied about their offering to the church, but we've all seen someone whose life was ruined because of a lack of honesty or financial integrity. Not everyone has seen a vision while banished on an island, been blinded by the truth that finally helps us see, been told to build a boat, rebuild a wall, or let someone else build a house for God. We all have different experiences—and yet, there are certain experiences, emotions, questions, and concerns that are common enough to be universal.

It's easy to see the things that make us different: race, gender, political affiliation, economic status, marital status; fit or fat, incarcerated or free, healthy or disabled. Yet there are some things that are common to the human family in every age and era. In *Preaching as Local Theology and Folk Art*, Leonora Tubbs Tisdale addresses these universal human experiences:

> Because people are, in certain respects, *like all others,* preachers can proclaim the gospel in a wide variety of settings with some assurance that (at least a degree of) effective, intelligible, and meaningful com-

munication can occur. It is the very assumption that people share common emotional experiences (anger, joy, frustration, or despair), biological characteristics (being born, helpless, needing food and drink for sustenance, aging, dying), or theological attributes (being created in the image of God, redeemed in Jesus Christ, and transformable through the workings of the Holy Spirit) that makes it possible for ministers to preach the gospel to people they do not know.[1]

The process of preaching preparation should include an examination of the text to see what is universal to the human condition. For example, take the story of Pentecost in Acts 2.

The list of universals could include: we have all been in a crowd; seen things we didn't know how to interpret; asked questions; felt or heard the wind; been drawn to something or someone; jumped to (false) conclusions; ridiculed something or someone we didn't understand. And of course, we all need to be saved, we all *can* be saved, and we all can be filled with the Holy Spirit.

There are other things in this text that are very specific to the people it describes: we have *not* all been to Jerusalem; made a pilgrimage for a religious festival; spoken in tongues; been drunk; or accepted a message about Jesus. While some among us may have had these experiences, we cannot call them universal.

The differentiation between universal and specific might seem insignificant, but if we want our preaching to be true to the text *and* connect with the people in front of us, we need to find common ground with everyone who's listening. That common ground is often found in universal human experiences.

When we preach specifics as universals, there will be people who think or say, *That's not true of me; I've never known what a good father is, argued about whether it was okay to drink, been to a hockey game, voted, held a baby, or been in a house with a group of Christians. That preacher obviously doesn't know anything about me. They're talking to someone who isn't like me—so maybe this whole message isn't for me.* People will stop listening to preachers who fail to

---

1. Tubbs Tisdale, *Preaching as Local Theology and Folk Art*, 11.

make authentic connections between the life of the text and the lives of the people in the congregation. They'll stop listening to a preacher who can't accurately assess both the text and the human condition. And once they stop listening, the opportunity for change, repentance, and redemption is gone. The whole sermon need not be built around universals, but making use of the universals in the text assures people that this word is for them. Universals bring a nod of recognition, and that nod keeps people listening.

Let's look at some examples of universals in a few texts.

Luke 1:26–38

The story of Jesus's birth has a rich array of universals. We have all been born; we all had a biological mother and father (whether we knew them or not); we all have a name; and we would all be afraid if an angel showed up and started talking to us. We've all been favored or graced; we've all been troubled by something we were told; we've all wondered what's next in a conversation; we've all been afraid; we've all asked "how?" We've all made a promise to someone; we've all had decisions made for us; we've all heard of someone who seemed too old or too young to have a baby. We've all questioned something that didn't seem possible, and we all must learn to submit to God.

1 Samuel 30

David and his men return from a deployment to find that that their base of operations has been burned to the ground and that their wives, children, and livestock have been carried away by the Amalekites. We all know stories of injustice; we've all felt like taking our pain out on someone else. We have all asked God for guidance when we've experienced loss, death, and grief over loved ones who were taken from us. We've all felt anger at those we have loved and to whom we've been loyal. We have all felt excitement or relief knowing our families were safe. We've all experienced difficulties or pain at home. We've all had enemies, have quickly gone from admiring someone to despising them, have been bitter in spirit, have needed to inquire of the Lord, have let down our guard, have felt like we couldn't go on, have been selfish or stingy, have needed a leader to get it right in a bad situation. We have all cried out to God, experienced triumphs, needed correction, received gifts, and been offered grace.

Universal experiences help bridge the gap between ancient texts and contemporary hearers. While they lived in a very different time and place, there are plenty of connections that can be made that make the people and God of the Bible more accessible and more relatable. It universally connects across time, culture, age, gender, and generation.

The flip side of identifying universals in human experience is being aware of the specific context in which we preach. As Leonora Tubbs Tisdale writes, "Parish pastors do not prepare their weekly sermons for generic humanity. They prepare sermons for particular individuals who populate their congregation and bring to the preaching event their own unique personalities, life circumstances, and concerns."[2] This is why, in our process of preparation, we should be attentive enough to note the universals in human experience while maintaining connections to the specific location and congregation in which we preach.

---

2. Tubbs Tisdale, *Preaching as Local Theology and Folk Art*, 11.

Sample Sermon: The Hope of Despair
Preached by Shawna Songer Gaines

Shawna Songer Gaines serves as chaplain at Trevecca Nazarene University in Nashville, Tennessee. The "aha" for this sermon came from an exploration of universals that led Shawna to consider the relationship between hope and despair. She preached this Palm Sunday text to a church in transition in Murfreesboro, Tennessee.

Luke 19:28–44

Hope and despair make curious traveling companions. But isn't that just what we see on the road covered with palms and garments?

There is such hopefulness among these disciples who have traveled with Jesus all the way to Jerusalem. In fact, they are so hopeful that they've staged a dramatization of a triumphal entry. You can't really call this a true triumphal entry when it's all wrong: there's no victory, no king, no power brokers, no drawn sword.

This is more of a creative reenactment—a kind of mock triumphal entry. The disciples have staged it at the back entrance of the city; perhaps there was a real king or dignitary using the main stage of the city gate. They draw a bit of a crowd among the religious scene (a few Pharisees at least), but none of the patrons of a real triumphal entry would be caught waving palm branches at a Galilean on a colt. Like children in their parents' suits, these glassy-eyed disciples put on their little play for the few who will humor them.

They get out their branches and take off their coats, though perhaps no one in Jerusalem will join them. And they shout the words of Psalm 118—"Blessed is the one who comes in the name of the Lord"—with such hope! This psalm sings about the love of God that endures forever. And these crazy disciples seem to honestly believe that Jesus has come to establish a kingdom that will last as long as the love of God.

My favorite part of Palm Sunday is when children wave palm branches in the sanctuary. My first Palm Sunday as a lead pastor, three weeks into a new assignment, I decided we would bring the children in to wave palms while we sang "Hosanna." There in California, we had real palm branches in abundance, and I didn't want to settle for the cheap plastic stuff. A gar-

PART 2: WHAT TO SAY

dener in the church told me he would have thirty real palms cut and ready at the front of the sanctuary on Palm Sunday morning. I was delighted.

On Palm Sunday morning I arrived to find five, seven-foot-long palm branches draped around the altar. Not only were they taller than the children, but if waved from the altar, they would reach back several pews! There was no time to trim them, and even if there had been, I didn't keep a chainsaw in my desk drawer.

"Hosanna" began, and the children were ushered in. You may have heard of the "splash zone" in the first five rows of a Sea World show. Well, on Palm Sunday at our church, the first three pews in the sanctuary were the "whack zone."

I wouldn't say that was my brightest moment in ministry, but it certainly stands out in the memory of the church—this young pastor and these adorable kids smacking their grandparents with palm branches. There was so much laughter, cuteness, joy—and, in a weird way, hope for the future.

The procession into Jerusalem is a messy, chaotic, unpolished scene filled with shouts and laughter and tears and so much hope. But in this procession of hope, despair is walking right alongside. You even hear it when the disciples say, "Peace in heaven, and glory in the highest heaven" (v. 38, NRSV). Familiar words—these bold disciples have rewritten the angels' song from Jesus's birth in Luke 2, when the whole company of heaven sang, "Glory to God in the highest heaven, and on earth peace to those on whom his favor rests" (v. 14).

At Jesus's birth—the hopeful beginning of what would be a sacrificial and hard journey—the angels up in heaven proclaim peace down on the earth. Thirty-three years later, Jesus's disciples on earth are looking at a messed-up Jerusalem, and they can only bear witness to peace in heaven. The disciples rewrite the angels' song in a way that makes sense on this journey—this journey of hope for what will be, mingled with despair at the world as it is.

And then, just in case we missed that hint of sorrow in the disciples' song of praise, Jesus looks at Jerusalem and bursts into tears. He weeps. And this hopeful procession is showered with the tears of despair. The reason he weeps is that they have not recognized "the things that make for peace" (19:42, ESV). Once again, we are forced to recognize that the peace the angels proclaimed that hopeful night in Bethlehem has yet to be realized in Jerusalem; in Nashville; in Murfreesboro; on earth.

Isn't peace often the sticking point between hope and despair?

Who doesn't hope for peace? In your life; your family; your workplace; in our city; our nation; our world? Who doesn't want to find a peaceful solution to the years-long civil war in Syria that has displaced 11 million people and killed hundreds of thousands? Who doesn't want to find a peaceful way to get through next week's Easter supper without having a shouting match with Uncle Bill? Who doesn't want to see more peaceful attitudes in our political discourse? Who doesn't want these things? We all do!

But this desire has become the butt of every Miss America joke. Only a silly girl parading around in heels and pearls would be naïve enough to say they actually hope for peace on earth. We are at a place in human history where it seriously seems more plausible to imagine humans colonizing another planet than being at peace with one another.

Peace has become a joke because we can't engineer it, calculate it, or script it. It is the frustrating glimmer of hope we've clung to for so long; and all we have to show for it is a whole lot of despair. Perhaps what is most frustrating is that the same violence and division that tear apart nations and peoples find a way to creep into our hearts as well.

As a preacher, I want so badly to tell you all about the hope of Easter that is victorious over the despairing grave—but that's not really fair; that's not really what we need to hear on Palm Sunday, and it's certainly not the message of Luke 19.

We must not miss the point here: this hopeful procession has *always* been leading to the cross. There is no hope in Easter without the utter despair of the cross. The cross is the place where hope goes to die.

Think about all those hopeful, bright-eyed, ragamuffin disciples who put on their silly drama at the back entrance to Jerusalem, their garments still dirty from being trampled by a little donkey colt. The Pharisees tried to warn them to stop their silly chants about Jesus being the king. But Jesus tells them to go on shouting, no matter how silly they might seem, if only to keep the rocks quiet for one more day. They finally get into Jerusalem where the real power brokers run the show. They arrive with their message of peace, the message of the kingdom of God, and they dare to break bread with this Jesus of Nazareth. They dare to stand with him when the guards come; some even support him at his trial. Their hope has brought them this far, but so few among them can bear to stand by while Jesus, their king who promised to usher in a new kingdom and a reign of peace, was hanged to die on a Roman cross—the cross that served as Rome's main instrument of peace by quieting the roaring mob.

On the cross, hope is crucified, and all they have left is deep, deep despair.

How do hopeful Christ followers walk the way of Jesus when the road is paved with despair? How do we hope for what Jesus taught us to pray—"Thy kingdom come . . . in earth, as it is in heaven" (Matthew 6:10, KJV)—when we are faced with the reality of the world as it is?

I think we often want to will ourselves past the despair and just push into hope so that we, in our own power, can somehow crush the despair that is crushing us. But that's like trying to walk down the road with only one leg, while dragging the other behind—it's just foolish, and it usually ends with an embarrassing fall.

Despair is not antithetical to Christian faith—we worship the Jesus who weeps over Jerusalem, who mourns the fate they have brought on him, who has been hurt so badly by his own people yet goes to the cross for them anyway. *He goes to the cross for them anyway!*

While thinking about and praying for you this week, and while praying over this passage, I couldn't help but think of what this might mean for you. I'm sure that individually, you each have stories of hope and despair—stories I couldn't imagine. But as a congregation, you are at a new place in your journey where the road ahead is unclear. A pastor loved and served you well for ten years, and you knew what life and ministry looked like under his shepherding; you don't know what lies ahead now. Perhaps there is some great hope for the future: hope in what God can do in a place and people like this; great hope for the people of Murfreesboro who don't yet know the peace of Christ that can transform a broken world; great hope for the children who wave palm branches today and for what they will do in the kingdom tomorrow.

But perhaps there is also some despair. In a congregation that is a hundred years old, I imagine you can point back to some glory days. Would you say that the world has changed a bit since those days? Would you say the church has changed? Change takes a lot of work; interim takes a lot of work. Reaching out to your community and hoping that they will respond—that requires you to put your heart and soul right out on your sleeve and invite them to be trampled. And maybe the sheer thought of it all is accompanied by some despair.

But can I tell you some good news: We've come to worship a King who knows a thing or two about despair. This King still walks with us on our journey of hope and despair. And there is no despair so deep that could drive Jesus away.

You see, the disciples were hopeful that Jesus would bring about peace like the kings they had seen in all those triumphal entry scenes—but Jesus wasn't one of those kings. When Jesus was crucified, hope died on a cross. Hope died, and some of those hopes needed to stay dead: hope for a king who would come with sword drawn, praised by all the power brokers of Jerusalem; hope for a peace that only served Jerusalem and cared nothing for the enemies at their door; hope that peace would give them an easy, Miss-America answer to all their big questions of life. Some of those things the disciples hoped for died on the cross and stayed dead—glory hallelujah!

Bring your hope to the cross: hope for the future; hope for all that might be; hope for good things, bad things, ugly things. Bring your hopes, nail them to the cross, and let them die. And as you stand before the death of your hopes, know that Christ is with you and that any of those hopes that look anything like Christ—any of those hopes that are truly from God—will come back to life. But the resurrection part is up to God, not you.

We don't know what will stay dead and what will be brought back to new life. But we do know that what God brings back to life will be marked by the peace of Christ—so you won't have to fight over it to preserve or protect it.

When you have been faithful to crucify your hopes and trust God with resurrection even in the face of despair, you can be sure that no matter what season of the journey you're walking through—one marked by hope or by despair—you will be able to join in the angels' song and proclaim for all the world to hear, "Glory to God in the highest, and on earth peace . . ." (Luke 2:14, ESV).

ten • TOOLS FOR ENGAGING THE TEXT: BAD NEWS

■ TROUBLE, or bad news, is not just part of the human experience; it's what gives us a reason to stay with a story. Trouble is a flat tire, pouring rain when the wedding is supposed to be outside, and a couple in their nineties given the promise of parenthood. Trouble is discrimination in the distribution of food to widows, stolen silver and garments buried under a tent. It's the oven going out on Thanksgiving morning, a prophet's wife going back to prostitution, a church that has lost its first love, an empty garden guarded by flaming swords. Trouble is Jonah going in the opposite direction, two men who fit the requirements for one replacement-disciple position, and two women in Philippi whose inability to get along affects the whole community.

Why would a preacher go looking for bad news in the text? Don't we see enough of that around us without looking for more in Scripture? The story of God involves a lot of trouble. If we humans are adept at anything, it is causing, exacerbating, and sometimes attempting to hide trouble. Sometimes the trouble in a text is easy to see: a giant is defying the army of Israel; Israel has made a golden calf; Judas has helped himself to the treasury.

Take for example, the story of the widow's offering in Mark 12:41–44. This brief scene is full of trouble: We (disciples/worshipers/leaders) judge by what we see, and what we see is the size of the offering but not the size of the sacrifice. This woman put in all she had to live on; what will happen to her now? Why didn't Jesus tell her to keep that offering for herself? Rich people are not able to give like poor widows. The lady was widowed. When death happens, we lose people we love. Loneliness is real. Poverty is present in the temple/church. The story ends with this woman's gift commended, but we have no idea what happens to her next. Even a scene as short as three verses can be saturated with trouble.

Another text that is full of trouble, especially when looking at the larger narrative in which it is found, is 2 Samuel 18, where we read about the death of Absalom. Trouble abounds in this story. King David's son is leading a rebellion that cannot be ignored. David tells three of his greatest killers—Joab, Abishai and Ittai—to "be gentle with the young man Absalom for my sake" (v. 5). There is relational trouble between David and Absalom, trouble for the nation because the king son's has divided loyalties, and trouble for Joab and those being asked to show mercy when that's not in their gift mix. David has set up a situation where it would be nearly impossible to have a win-win. The rebellion can be put down, but David also wants mercy for the rebel.

The gospel isn't written for perfect people in a problem-free world. In fact, sometimes the message of the gospel *is* the trouble that causes people dismay (as in the story of the rich young ruler). The Bible deals with real people, families, communities, and political structures that are full of bad news. Sometimes the reality of evil is so palpable in Scripture that we can see, hear, smell, taste, and touch it.

Abraham lied about his wife. Elijah got depressed. Daniel was thrown into a pit. Ruth became a widow. Following Jesus led to persecution, imprisonment, and even death for early believers. Two super-Christians, Paul and Barnabas "had such a sharp disagreement that they parted company" (Acts 15:39). The church had to deal with heresy.

The Bible and the world in which we live are both full of trouble. We don't help anyone by minimizing the reality of evil or trouble—whether we find it in the text or experience it in ministry. To pretend that trouble doesn't exist, or to slap weak platitudes on bad news, is to make light of the heaviness the Bible addresses and the heaviness our congregations live. It's hard to make the good news sound as good as it really is when we haven't been honest about how bad the bad news really is. The Bible does not shy away from the reality of evil or from the pain, suffering, and misery that sin causes—and neither should we. When you go to the text, look for trouble; you probably won't have to look far.

For example, let's take a look at the trouble displayed in the following passages:

Psalm 64

This psalm is full of trouble. David's enemies are threatening him. There's a conspiracy. People are wicked, ruthless evildoers; they attack the innocent and feed on each other's evil; they are arrogant and proud in their schemes; they plot injustice. Nothing in David's description is sugarcoated. He gives voice to the trouble with vivid images: "They sharpen their tongues like swords and aim cruel words like deadly arrows" (v. 3). The text will move to good news but not before thoroughly imaging the reality of evil.

Luke 15:11–32

Bad news is everywhere in the story of the prodigal son. The son disrespects his father. His friends run out when the money runs out. He makes decisions he can't unmake and wastes days he can't get back. Pigpens stink and aren't meant for people, but the prodigal son still ends up there. While the prodigal son does his sinning abroad, the other son does his sinning without ever leaving home. The older brother was close to the father, but he still didn't understand his father's heart. Not everyone celebrates when the sinner comes home, and we never find out whether the older brother joined the party.

One of the beautiful things about Scripture is that the trouble in it is true to life. Sometimes trouble, or tension, is resolved fairly quickly. Other times it lasts a long time and, in some cases, may not resolve at all. But God is present when humans get into trouble. God is at work, even—or maybe especially—in bad-news situations. Preachers who give serious attention to bad news in the text will never want for ways to connect the ancient text with the modern hearer because we all know the reality of evil. We've all experienced bad news. We've all been not only around trouble but *in* it. Great preachers know how to make the most of the bad news in the text—and how to make the good news so good that it overwhelms the bad. We'll turn our attention to that shortly, but first let's take a look in the next chapter at a masterful, first-ever sermon that was birthed by asking the question, "Where is the bad news?"

■ ■ ■
Sample Sermon:
A Communal Call to Parenting
Preached by Robert Breddin

In a preaching class at Nazarene Theological Seminary, Rev. Robert Breddin prepared his first-ever sermon using the process described in this book. His "aha" moment came one night when the bad news in the text connected with bad news in our own world—the increasing problem of fatherlessness. Robert preached this sermon to a class of preachers-in-the-making.

Matthew 1:18–25

Joseph is like many of you sitting here today, and like many in your congregation. He comes from a line of farmers, shepherds, pastors, people of power, businessmen and businesswomen. He even has some family members he doesn't like to talk about too much (you know what I mean).

Joseph works hard, and like everyone else, he has big hopes and dreams for the future. His parents have arranged for his marriage to a nice, godly young woman. Their betrothal has been announced before witnesses; the bride price has been paid; the dowry has been arranged. His buddies are patting him on his back, congratulating him, telling him all about the joys of married life. Everything seems to be going well for Joseph.

Then everything—*his* hopes, *his* plans—it all falls to pieces. Mary turns up pregnant, and she's saying that *God* is the father. Even though Joseph feels crushed, betrayed, and heartbroken, he's a righteous man and does not want to disgrace her. So he plans to send her away secretly.

Joseph is probably wondering what he's going to do now. But God has his own plan: The angel of the Lord appears to Joseph in a dream and tells him, "Do not be afraid to take Mary as your wife; for the Child who has been conceived in her is of the Holy Spirit" (v. 20, NASB). At this moment, Joseph has serious suspicions about Mary, and he *certainly* has trust issues. But still, he trusts this special revelation from the angel of the Lord.

Make no mistake—even though the angel commanded Joseph to take Mary as his wife, he did not *have* to marry her. He had free will; he still could have sent her away. But Joseph trusted God and married her by faith, trusting that God would work it out for his good. He chose to obey

PART 2: WHAT TO SAY

what the Lord asked him to do; and, because of that, he is forever remembered as the earthly father of our Lord Jesus Christ.

If we stand back and look at the text, we notice that Joseph immediately obeyed God. He did not take weeks to think about it—he immediately agreed to raise a child who was not his own. This made him responsible for providing food, clothing, and education for a child who was not from his own seed. But Joseph, being a righteous man, cared for Jesus as if he were his own.

There are many people in the world today who take on the responsibility of raising children who are not their own. They might adopt, serve as foster parents, or help raise kids from their husband or wife's previous marriage. Others might serve as mentors, or as Big Brothers and Big Sisters in the community. As pastors, many of you will be seen as parental figures; you'll be called to serve as mothers and fathers to children whose parents aren't around. In the process, you will grow to love those children as your own. And *yes*—when you are put in these situations, you will be afraid, just like Joseph was!

The angel of the Lord told Joseph that this baby was conceived by the Holy Spirit and that he would save his people from their sins. So we can assume that Joseph realized this child was special. Like Joseph, we should assume that all kids are special. They may not be Holy-Spirit-conceived, but they are Holy-Spirit-breathed. They may not be God, but they are made in his image. Sometimes it might be hard to remember that. I spent many years working in a classroom as a teacher, and I'll tell you—sometimes it seems like they're made in the other guy's image.

How is God leading you to help children? Again, some of you may be called to foster or adopt, or perhaps the Lord will lead you to marry someone who has kids from a previous marriage. In many cases, it might simply mean keeping an eye out, giving a hand up, or sharing an encouraging word. It might mean supporting other people who work with kids. Like Joseph, you are all righteous; if not, let me introduce you to the one who can make you righteous. Children are some of the most vulnerable people in our society, and I know that we are all called to take part in helping them.

Even though Joseph knew the child was conceived of the Holy Spirit, he may have felt disappointed that his firstborn child was not his own offspring. He didn't even get the opportunity to name the child Joseph Jr., or any other name he might have picked out—instead, the angel told him to name the child *Immanuel*. Even though the circumstances were nothing like what Joseph had planned, he rose above any disappointment he may have felt, and obeyed God.

God may also ask you to look after his little creations in ways that don't fit into your plans for your life or ministry. Can you rise above the disappointment and, by faith, obey God? I would also like to point out here that Joseph *was* obeying a command from God in all this—so, for major decisions related to children, make sure you are doing the will of God.

Joseph showed remarkable character in planning to handle the situation with Mary discreetly, in obeying the angel's instructions to marry her, and in conducting himself as a godly man throughout. Likewise, in our churches, we are placed in an ideal position to rise up as a community and care for children who are not our own. We have an opportunity to form a godly community that sees kids as God's wonderful creations and to support and demonstrate holiness to parents and their children.

In Joseph's case, he will be recognized throughout eternity as the earthly father of Jesus; *our* actions have eternal implications as well. One day, when you are in heaven, the kids you helped might come up to you and say, "You told me about Jesus and taught me how to play tennis"; "You taught me how to be a godly woman while my mom was in jail"; "You believed in me and helped me become a Bible quizzing champion"; "You helped me repair my first car after my dad died."

Just as Joseph did with Jesus, when you teach and care for God's children, you are bringing the kingdom of God to earth in a tangible way.

eleven • TOOLS FOR ENGAGING THE TEXT: GOOD NEWS

■ AT SOME point, someone taught me that it's not a Christian sermon unless there is good news. I agree wholeheartedly (with the rare exception, as we saw in the sample sermon by Dan Boone). As a young preacher, sharing good news was probably my biggest weakness. My sermons were like too many testimonies I've heard: fifteen minutes of detailed, vividly narrated bad news, and about fifteen seconds of good news that didn't have enough weight to swallow the bad news. When it comes to testimonies, bad news is interesting. At times, it can be downright fascinating. It's hard to picture that sweet old lady as a promiscuous rebel or that gray-haired saint as an alcoholic. But as Paul writes in 1 Corinthians 6:11, "That is what some of you were."

As a young preacher, it was much easier for me to find bad news to rail against than it was to find good news to inspire. But the good news must be more than sounded—it must be big enough to overcome the bad news, just as the resurrection of Jesus swallowed up the power of sin and death.

If you write a manuscript during your sermon preparation (and I hope you do), look at the pages—how many lines, paragraphs, or pages are devoted to good news? Where are there sprinkles of grace? If it's fifteen minutes of bad news and fifteen seconds of, "But Jesus can make it better," that's not enough good news. Let grace abound! How good do you make the good news?

It's worth the effort to find ways to articulate, share, and experience the good news in your sermon. Think about all the good-news words, images, songs, and stories in the Bible. Reflect on your own experiences of God's grace. Where have you seen light defeat darkness, good overcome evil? When have you seen God prove himself to be your rock, refuge, restorer, reconciler, redeemer? In every text, ask the question, "Where is the grace?" Where is the good news? You'll find it—because it's there. I promise.

We can see the good news at work in the following sample passages.

Matthew 11:2–6

John the Baptist asks whether Jesus is the Messiah. John is raising this question while he is in prison—yet the text is full of grace and good news, showing us that even people as faithful as John the Baptist experience doubt, and that Jesus isn't offended by our questions. This text teaches us that the blind see, the lame walk, lepers are healed, the deaf hear, the dead are raised, and the good news is proclaimed to the poor. Jesus doesn't scold, chastise, berate, or condemn John for questioning or doubting him, and he won't blame us for our questions either.

Matthew 7:21–29

In this troubling text, we learn that not everyone who says to Jesus, "Lord, Lord," will enter the kingdom of heaven. That's bad news. Yet there is still good news here: fakes will ultimately be revealed for what they are. In the parable of the house built on the rock, we find more good news: we can choose God as our solid foundation; we can know God and do God's will; we can withstand storms. And we can trust what Jesus tells us because he speaks with authority that is from heaven.

Jesus tells us exactly how he expects us to live a kingdom life *now* so that we are and will be included in the kingdom of heaven. This text shows us that God will reveal his will to us if we are in tune with him and that a relationship with Christ *does* matter in the long run. Building on the rock of the foundation of God is an option that is open to everyone. That's good news!

Luke 10:25–37

Jesus's parable of the Good Samaritan is full of good news. To start, Jesus engages in the conversation even though the expert in the law approaches him with bad motives. In the parable, we learn that we can *be* good neighbors and *have* good neighbors. We learn that we are to consider everyone our neighbor and that real love is demonstrated through actions. Additionally, we learn that even "bad guys" (as the Jews characterized the Samaritans) can choose to be good guys.

■ ■ ■
Sample Sermon: Bring It In!
Preached by Steve Estep

It can be difficult to preach a list of ethical admonitions. In order to make it anything other than a works-righteousness, pull-yourself-up-by-your-bootstraps, behavior-modification sermon, the good news has to be good. And if the response is going to be anything other than a guilt-induced attempt to straighten up our act, the good news must also be big. The sermon must be grounded in the good news that God empowers the kind of holy life that God demands. I attempted to do that in this sermon.

Ephesians 4:20–5:2

It was nearing 6:00 p.m., and the Tennessee sun was still hot enough to make the sweat run down my spine even as I stood still. The Rossview High School football team had been at it for three hours when the whistle blew to signal it was time to bring it in. The head coach, my friend Ron Lambert, positioned himself where each of the hundred-plus players could see him without having to look into the sun. "Tomorrow is the first day of school," he said.

What followed was a list of dos and don'ts that rivaled one of the apostle Paul's rapid-fire vice-and-virtue lists: "Don't be late. Dress well. You don't need to wear your jersey to let girls know you're on the team—they don't care anyway. I expect every one of you to look respectable. No saggy pants, and leave your hats at home. Keep your hands to yourselves. Don't be touching anybody" (and he elaborated on that one a bit). "We say 'yes sir' and 'no sir,' not 'yep' and 'uh-uh.' Respect everyone in authority, from the custodians to the principal. If someone else messes up, it doesn't get any press. If one of you does, it's not '3.0 student makes bad decision,' it's 'Rossview football player . . .' You represent RHS football, and we have an image to maintain."

Ron wasn't just reminding the players how to behave—he was reminding them who they were. It was a sort of "live a life worthy of the call" speech. At different times he looked players in the eye (like pastors are tempted to do when hitting certain points in their sermons). His words were fitting for those boys he knew well, but I think they could easily apply to any team.

Sample Sermon: Steve Estep

It makes me wonder: when Paul wrote to the church in Ephesus, did he just have a good understanding of humanity in general, or was he aware of specific issues the saints there were dealing with? I imagine he *did* know the Ephesians pretty well, but even so, I think his words of wisdom are applicable to every other group of saints, including us. (And yes, that label fits us too—saints, created to be like Jesus in righteousness and holiness.)

When Paul's letter arrived, it alerted the saints that it was time to bring it in. So they circled up to hear what Paul had to say and what God had to say through him. Paul spent the first half of the letter reminding the Ephesians who they were, who they had become in Christ, and how they'd gotten there. He spent the second half telling them how to behave. But in calling the Ephesians to specific practices of holy living, Paul was not saying, "You have an image to uphold." Rather, he was saying, "You have an image in which you were made—in fact, you were created to be like Christ in righteousness and holiness. And with that comes a different way of life. You need to learn it, and I'm here (in letter form, at least) to help you figure it out."

When I imagine that group in Ephesus, I imagine that, like every other group of saints, the only reason they had for being together, the only thing they had in common, was their relationship with Jesus.

I picture a guy named Ephraim. He's a camel salesman, gifted in the art of embellishment and selective recall when it comes to the poor-health history of his stock. He's always justified his shady ways by reminding himself that he has a family to feed. So if he happens to overestimate the quality or underestimate the liabilities of his product, well . . .

Half-truths and deception have become so woven into the fabric of his life that even since he came to faith in Jesus, he's struggled with truthfulness. And it's not just at work—a habit like deception doesn't tend to stay confined. It's not that he sets out to lie to the people he loves, but many of his conversations aren't exactly "the whole truth and nothing but the truth."

But when Ephraim hears Paul's words, "put off falsehood and speak truthfully to your neighbor" (4:25), it's like he can feel Paul's gaze through the page. The Holy Spirit is all over him. About that time, he glances across the room and sees a brother he recently tricked into buying some bad stock.

Up to that point, Ephraim has always received the Word he's heard. There's no doubt he's a man of faith and that he's had a genuine experience with Jesus Christ. But he knows that this unholy practice of deception is incompatible with the righteousness and holiness of God, and he knows he's going to have to deal with it. But how? How could he ever overcome such a deeply ingrained behavior?

I imagine that among those listening to Paul's letter are parents who feel convicted when they hear, "'In your anger do not sin': Do not let the sun go down while you are still angry, and do not give the devil a foothold" (4:26). The saintly couple haven't talked to each other in two days. It's not for lack of opportunity—however, neither is willing to give or receive an apology. There hasn't been any yelling, but the anger has come out in different ways: clanged dishes, slammed doors, cold shoulders, harsh looks. They didn't invent these ways of dealing with their emotions; they're simply following the examples they've been given. But now their actions are starting to affect the next generation.

Just that morning they watched their toddler mirror the temper tantrums she's been seeing. She looked straight at them when she slammed the door to her dollhouse, as if to say, "Is that how you do it, Mom and Dad?" They both struggle to find ways to deal with their anger, and now, at this gathering of the saints, they are confronted with their own behaviors—behaviors that are incompatible with the righteousness and holiness of God. The habits are too ingrained to be easily broken. And while they know Paul's words are right, they wonder how they can ever deal with their anger without sinning. Their whole mindset will have to change.

Maria has no problems with dishonesty or with anger. But before she came to faith in Christ, it was common that when she left a room, she carried out more than she'd brought in. This was more out of necessity than malice; she'd been forced to take care of herself since she was fourteen years old. She'd learned to be resourceful not because she wanted to be but because she had to be. She'd never been in a position to give, only to take, to survive. When she heard Paul's admonition not only to stop stealing but also to work hard enough to have something to give others, it felt like he was asking the impossible. How deep could this transformation go? How righteous and holy could she really become?

As the circle of saints continue listening to the letter, the virtues and vices come at them one by one: "Do not let any unwholesome talk come out of your mouths, but only what is helpful for building others up . . . Get rid of bitterness, rage and anger . . . Be kind and compassionate to one another, forgiving each other" (vv. 29, 31–32). One by one the items on the list take root in their hearts, calling them to Christlike lives, reminding them that they have an image not to uphold but to live into—the image of God.

About this time, someone says what they're all thinking: "How? How can this really be? We're not super-disciples like Paul. We're common people with everyday problems, wearing the scars of our own sins and the sins committed against us. How can this really happen?"

Then the reader gets everyone's attention: "Didn't you hear it? Listen to this again:"

1:4

"For he chose us in him before the creation of the world to be holy and blameless in his sight." *We were chosen for this life.*

4:23–24

"Be made new in the attitude of your minds; and . . . put on the new self, created to be like God in true righteousness and holiness." *We were created for this life.*

2:21–22

"In him the whole building is joined together and rises to become a holy temple in the Lord. And in him you too are being built together to become a dwelling in which God lives by his Spirit." *It's already happening.* I mean, think about it—how many of us ever imagined we'd see as much change as we've seen already? None of us!

"And there's more!" the reader says. "Throughout the letter, Paul doesn't just instruct us—he prays for us too."

1:18–19

Paul prays that we would know the Spirit's power, the same power that raised Jesus from the dead.

3:16

Paul prays for power "through his Spirit in your inner being."

3:18

He prays that you "may have power, together with all the Lord's holy people, to grasp how wide and long and high and deep is the love of Christ, and to know this love that surpasses knowledge—that you may be filled to the measure of all the fullness of God."

3:20

The benediction is beautiful: "Now to him who is able to do immeasurably more than all we ask or imagine, according to his power that is at work within us, to him be glory in the church and in Christ Jesus throughout all generations, for ever and ever! Amen."

"I get it!" says one of the saints. "The same Spirit who raised Jesus from the dead is the one who lives in us, renews our minds so we have the mind of Christ, and gives us his power so we can live holy lives that reflect the image we were created in. Maybe we should start praying for ourselves what Paul prays for us: 'God, I want to be consumed with the same Spirit that raised Jesus from the dead, that recreates me and empowers me. I want the power of your Spirit to be so at work in me that my words are always truth, my anger doesn't lead to sin, and my old habits no longer master me . . .'"

And maybe it's a good time for us do the same. "Jesus, I want and need your Spirit's all-consuming power to help me live this holy life for which I was created. Amen."

twelve • TOOLS FOR ENGAGING THE TEXT: POINTS OF VIEW

■ **IN 2008,** Sony Pictures released a film called *Vantage Point*. The setting is a counter-terrorism summit in Spain at which the president of the United States is scheduled to speak. Shortly after stepping onto the podium, the president is shot by a would-be assassin, and pandemonium breaks out. Throughout the rest of the movie, that scene is repeated eight times, each time from the perspective (or vantage point) of a different witness.

As I watched that film, I thought about preaching. There are multiple points of view in most biblical texts. There are the primary characters themselves, of course. Many times, there are crowds of people that contain perspectives from all ages and backgrounds. Sometimes we get a blast from the past as Old Testament prophets are referenced in New Testament conversations. The story of the woman caught in adultery looks different to the woman than it does to the line-drawing, stone-clutching religious leaders. It looks different to her unnamed partner than it does to the disciples who are with Jesus as the scene unfolds. With each point of view, the story sounds and feels different. Well-worn stories can spark fresh insights when we adopt the perspective of a character with whom we wouldn't normally identify.

I have heard some incredible sermons that unleashed old texts in new ways simply by changing the point of view. When I was in seminary, I took a preaching class at Saint Paul School of Theology precisely because Eugene Lowry was the professor. In that course, one of my classmates preached on Jesus's parable of the wandering sheep. She spoke from the perspective of some of the ninety-nine who were unhappy that the shepherd had left them to search for their stray brother. In the voices of these sheep, we heard the voices of those who are safely inside the church, who blame the lost for being lost, who fault the shepherd for abandoning the well-behaved sheep who deserve better than to be left alone. I've never read that story the same way since. It was a masterful, insightful, Spirit-inspired sermon. The text came alive in a new way because the preacher helped us adopt a different perspective.

Why not tell the story of the temple cleansing in John 2 from the perspective of the custodian who had to clean up the mess? In Galatians, how would Paul's beef with the Judaizers appear to someone who had committed their entire life to upholding orthodoxy as they knew it? What about when David danced before the ark of the covenant as it was brought to Jerusalem (2 Samuel 6)—ever thought about telling that story from the perspective of Michal, the disapproving wife? How would the story of David and Goliath sound from the perspective of Goliath or another Philistine soldier? What if we looked at a confrontation between Jesus and the Pharisees from the Pharisees' point of view?

In my process of preparation, I ask these point-of-view questions not just to spark my imagination but also to challenge my familiarity with the well-traveled roads through some very rich scriptures. This exercise can take a few minutes, or it may sometimes take a little longer. But however long it takes you, the time spent will be well worth it. After all, the call to preach is the call to prepare, and preparation takes time.

Sample Sermon: Here's Lookin' at You
Preached by Jeremy Byler

Jeremy Byler is associate pastor at Erin Church of the Nazarene in Erin, Tennessee. He was a student in one of my preaching classes and now works primarily with children and families. In the sermon that follows, you will see how he adopts the perspectives of a few different people from the text in Mark where Jesus blesses the same children his disciples rebuke. Using dialogical language, Jeremy taps into a variety of viewpoints and offers insights we might otherwise miss. His sermon content is based on the points-of-view tool, but his structure is from Paul Scott Wilson's The Four Pages of the Sermon.

Mark 10:13–16; Deuteronomy 6:4

Introduction

If your children will become you, who or what will they become?

Why do we bring our children to Jesus? Do we really believe that he can change, impact, and use them now? Or is this just what we do? Do we really believe that Jesus has time for our crazy kids? Do we take the time to share what we know about Jesus with them? Are our kids catching *our* excitement and passion for Jesus?

Our kids tend to get excited about the things we're excited about. They will honor the things we honor and value the things we value. When I was a kid, my favorite music was country gospel and southern gospel—groups like The King's Men, The Blackwood Brothers, and The Maranatha Singers. I loved to sing those songs with my parents. This was their favorite kind of music, so it became my favorite—at least until I got a little older. Though my taste in music has changed many times in the years since, there is still a sweet place in my heart for the songs I sang with Mom and Dad when I was young.

You don't have to be a perfect parent. You don't have to know the Bible cover to cover. Just start by opening it up. Kids don't need you to be a theologian! You can't do everything—just do something! Start by bringing your kids to Jesus! Start by showing your children Jesus!

Story

Imagine how that day unfolded for the families who had come to see Jesus. I'd like to propose that perhaps there were two different kinds of families there on that day.

For one family, the day starts out in a rush. Mom is running through the house getting the kids ready to go; she's cleaned their faces and dressed them in something nice. Dad is sitting at the table eating breakfast, still trying to wake up, not really ready himself. All the while, Mom and Dad are debating whether this is really the way they want to spend their day.

Dad says, "Come on! You know I was supposed to go fishing with the guys today, and I'm going to the temple tomorrow. Is this really necessary?"

Mom's reply is less than convincing: "Oh come on, Thaddeus. I was talking to Beth at the well yesterday and they're taking their kids, so we need to go too! I don't want to be the only one who didn't take their kids to see this guy. I heard he's only staying for a little while, and who knows when he'll be in the area again."

You can imagine Dad's reaction: "Oh, I see—you've been talking to Beth again."

Mom says, "Come on, Thaddeus! She says there's something different about this guy."

Dad begrudgingly agrees, throws on some clothes decent enough to wear in public, and begins addressing the kids: "We're going to meet someone very important today, and you need to be on your best behavior. You're not to speak unless spoken to. You're going to stand still and stay right beside us until it's time."

The little girl pipes up and says, "Time for what, Daddy?"

"Don't worry about it," Dad says. Under his breath, he mutters, "Not like it's going to matter anyway." And they head off.

Family number two starts the day with an early breakfast around the table. Every one of them has goose bumps as they look forward to the events of the day. For a few days, Mom and Dad have been telling the kids that something special will happen today—something that could change their lives forever.

The kids are being kids, wiggling and giggling as they mill about the house getting ready to go. The oldest son sidles up to Dad, who is waiting outside for the rest of the family, and asks, "Dad, are we really going to meet Jesus today?"

The dad looks back at his son and says, "Yes, we are taking you to meet Jesus."

"Dad, is it true that he made a blind man able to see? Is it true that he fed all those people with only two fish and five loaves of bread?"

"Of course it's true, son. Why would I lie to you? Don't you know that I love you?"

"Well, yeah, Dad, I know you love me, but some of the other kids say it was just a trick—that the blind guy was faking, and they already had the baskets of food ready to feed those people. But it wasn't a trick, was it? He really does miracles, doesn't he?"

"Son," the dad says, "This man is more than a man. He's more than a healer, and he's more than a teacher. He is the Son of God—the Messiah. And we are taking you kids today to be blessed by him."

"Why, Dad? I'm not sick."

"Son, your mother and I are taking you to see Jesus not because you're sick, not because you need a miracle, but because we believe he is the Messiah. Beyond that, I don't know what to expect. I don't know what it will mean for you to have his blessing. All I know is that if he really is the Son of God, that changes everything. I want you to meet him now, while you are young and willing to learn."

Just then the other kids burst out of the house, grinning from ear to ear, and they head off.

The Journey

So these families have started on their journey to see Jesus, and I have to ask: do they really know why they're going? Do they know whom they're taking their children to meet? Do they realize they're taking their children to the one who holds life and death in his hands? The one who knit each of those children together in their mothers' wombs? Do they realize that when they take their children to Jesus, they are taking them to one who has not only seen their future but has also set it in motion? Do they know that when they ask for their children to be blessed, they're asking the one who is the reason for their very existence? Or are they bringing their children in hopes they'll be blessed with health, wealth, and good fortune? Are they coming to get their kids autographed by the latest religious rock star? Whatever the case, they are doing the right thing by bringing their children to Jesus.

Imagine the gathering of people as they begin to draw near to where Jesus is. Imagine that, as these two families walk side by side up the crowded road, the oldest sons begin to talk. They exchange some greetings, names maybe, and a complaint about a younger sibling. The boy from the first family asks the other boy who exactly they're going to see and why everyone thinks it's such a big deal.

"We're going to meet the Messiah."

"The who?"

"The Messiah—Jesus."

"Oh, Jesus . . . Jesus . . . nope, never heard of the guy."

Now the other boy is getting a little excited. "*Never heard of the guy?*"

"Shhh! No, I've never heard of him. What's the big deal?"

The young man shares everything he knows about Jesus, recounting his earlier conversation with his dad. Now both boys are bubbling with excitement to meet this Jesus.

The Children

I think we've all seen the storybook pictures of wide-eyed, smiling boys and girls sitting on Jesus's lap—nice, clean preschoolers dressed in church clothes, with pretty little bows in their hair.

As the two families get closer to the place where Jesus will be speaking, I think it's probably more like kids of all ages with lunch stains on their faces and clothes. Some kids probably smell like the fish they just ate. I'm sure there are some dirty diapers in the bunch. And there's probably a baby or two who's more concerned about getting fed than with sitting quietly. I'm sure this was not a peaceful, breezy scene under an olive tree. Because let's be honest: when there are kids in the mix, their excitement, curiosity, and natural energy—everything that makes them kids—comes out in ways that, to the untrained ear, sound a little like chaos. There are squeals, giggles, tears, shouts. I'm sure there's tussling between siblings as they try to determine who will be first in line. And there may be some older kids, even teenagers, who come with smells and emotions of their own.

Sample Sermon: Jeremy Byler

Trouble in the Scripture: Disciples

So as Jesus appears on the scene, he isn't walking into a quiet group of adults seated nicely with their hands folded in their laps, waiting to be taught. No, he walks into a bit of a circus. There is probably a hush as the kids begin to whisper, "Is that him?"

And then it happens—one little guy just can't take it anymore. He pushes and squirms his way through the crowd and heads right for Jesus, running all the way down. He stops right at his feet, looks up with an ear-to-ear grin, and just stares at him. Of course, as soon as one kid goes, they all break loose—a mob of pure energy running straight for their Creator.

Then, out of nowhere, like Kevin Costner in *The Bodyguard*, Peter and the other disciples come flying in and scoop up the little boy and all the others, pushing them back toward the crowd, rebuking them. *Rebuking!* That's a strong word. The disciples don't just say, "No, no, kids, go back to Mommy." To rebuke is to show sharp, stern disapproval; to reprove or reprimand. The disciples are beside themselves; there is an attitude of *how dare they!*

Why would the disciples react like that to these children? Perhaps they're thinking, *Are you serious? Where are these kids' parents? Don't you know who this is? This is the Messiah! You can't just run up to Jesus! He's not interested in playing tag. You can't play rodeo on his knee or have a piggyback ride. No, wait—that one has boogers! This is God's Son! They might get him dirty, smelly. Are these kids even clean?*

Or maybe the disciples think that Jesus is just too busy for this. He's talking about some deep spiritual stuff here! It's only a matter of time before they move on to the next town, and it's important for Jesus to be able to preach as much as possible. These kids can't understand what Jesus is talking about—let him focus on the adults. He doesn't have *time* to deal with these kids.

Here's my question: why don't the disciples rebuke the parents? Bringing the children was *their* idea, wasn't it? Verse 13 says, "People were bringing little children to Jesus." It doesn't say, "One day, a whole gang of kids decided to find Jesus and see if he'd like to play." So why don't the disciples holler at the parents to grab their kids and then lecture the parents about why this is inappropriate? I'm guessing it's because they don't want to offend potential listeners. So instead, they rebuke the children—they're just kids; adults can speak to them or treat them however they want, right? They need to learn respect. Children are to be seen, not heard.

I wonder if the disciples even know why the children have come, or if that would make a difference. I don't know exactly what it is that causes the disciples to rebuke the kids, but they do.

Trouble in the Real World

There's a problem here: in the real world, there are parents who are constantly rebuking their kids. Parents rebuke their kids because they're so wrapped up in pleasing themselves that their children come second, or third, or fourth. Sometimes kids are rebuked for even existing.

Single parents might rebuke their children when they look at them and see their former spouse. When they remember the unplanned pregnancy, the pain of the partner who walked away, they might rebuke their children by telling them they were a mistake. Children are rebuked when Mom or Dad refuses to seek help for an addiction. Kids are rebuked when they spend entire weekends scrounging for food because adults have partied so hard they won't wake up for days—and maybe when they do wake up, the kids run and hide so they won't be beaten. Kids are rebuked when there's a different man or woman sleeping in their house every week. They're rebuked when their hygiene isn't looked after properly. Children are rebuked when they are raised by television and the internet because Mom and Dad have chosen other pursuits. Parents who rebuke their children don't even always know they're doing it, and don't always do it on purpose, but it happens when choices are made that do not prioritize the well-being and healthy growth of children.

What then becomes of these kids who have been rebuked? They are left to raise themselves. They might pattern their lives after people they see on TV or the internet. Eventually, they may realize that not everyone can be a celebrity, a rock star, or a pro athlete. They are left with few hopes, unfulfilled dreams, and unhealthy role models. So these children may eventually become their parents, and then they may have their own children, and—because they weren't taught a better way—they might end up rebuking their children too, and the cycle will continue.

Sample Sermon: Jeremy Byler

Grace in the Scripture

The good news in this text is that Jesus doesn't let the disciples get away with rebuking the children. The NIV says that Jesus is "indignant" at the disciples' unjust actions. The Message translation says he is "irate." Jesus can't believe that the disciples would treat these children like this. He has to be thinking, *Didn't we just go over this when you were arguing about who was the greatest (Mark 9:33–36)? Didn't I put a child in front of you and say, 'Whoever welcomes one of these little children in my name welcomes me' (v. 37)? What are you thinking?*

Jesus, with love in his eyes and compassion in his heart, reaches out his hands and says, "'Let the little children come to me, and do *not* hinder them, for the kingdom of God belongs to such as these. Truly I tell you, anyone who will not receive the kingdom of God like a little child will never enter it.' And he took the children in his arms, placed his hands on them and blessed them" (10:14–16).

Jesus does something incredible here. He not only takes a typical disciple-style mistake and turns it into a teaching moment, but he also makes a declaration: "Let the little children come to me, and *do not hinder them*! Do not keep them from me! Do not fill them with false information about me! Do not hinder these children by filling their minds with the garbage and false hope this world has to offer. Do not hinder these children by making them raise themselves. Do not hinder them by letting rock stars and celebrities tell them what to think about life, love, sex, and drugs. Do not hinder them by allowing or forcing them to take part in adult perversion. Do not hinder them by letting their schedules be their god! Do not hinder these children by neglecting to play an active role in their physical and spiritual lives! Do not rebuke these children for the sake of the 'people who really matter'—the businesspeople, the athletes, the celebrities, the politicians. The kingdom of heaven does not belong to those people! It belongs to the children. So do not rebuke them! Bring them to me!"

Then Jesus takes the children into his arms, places his hands on them, and blesses them. Jesus says, "Bring them to me. I will take them in my arms, and I will bless them! Bring them to me."

Grace in the Real World

Have you brought your kids to Jesus, or have you only brought your kids to church? What does it look like to bring your kids to Jesus? You say, "I bring them to *you*, Pastor Jeremy! That's what it looks like! You said I'm no theologian! I'm still kind of new at this myself—how am I supposed to bring my kids to Jesus?"

What does it look like? It looks like a mom and dad who say a simple prayer with their kids when they tuck them in at night. It looks like a family singing Christmas songs in the car because the same album has been playing for eight weeks straight and everyone knows the words! It looks like a family sitting down to dinner together and talking about the day, and then giving thanks to Jesus for all the good things they have. It looks like Tommy sneaking out of his bed at night to find Mom and Dad praying together and taking their concerns to God rather than fighting. It looks like being involved in the life and service of the church; being faithful with your finances; praising God when things are good; trusting God when things are difficult; loving others and putting them first. Bringing your children to Jesus looks like running to Jesus yourself.

The *Shema*, which is what we call a portion of Scripture found in Deuteronomy 6, is a very important piece of Scripture in Jewish culture. It was the scripture God's people used to ensure that the story of God, their traditions, and their identity were passed from generation to generation. The *Shema* says: "Hear, O Israel: The Lord our God, the Lord is one. Love the Lord your God with all your heart and with all your soul and with all your strength. These commandments that I give you today are to be on your hearts. Impress them on your children. Talk about them when you sit at home and when you walk along the road, when you lie down and when you get up. Tie them as symbols on your hands and bind them on your foreheads. Write them on the doorframes of your houses and on your gates" (vv. 4–9).

That's it. Parents, there is incredible encouragement here. This text doesn't say, "Bring your child to the temple and the priests will teach them everything they need to know—just leave it to the professionals." It doesn't say, "Make sure that you memorize the whole Bible from cover to cover and teach your kids the Articles of Faith while on vacation." It says to love the Lord with all your heart, soul, and strength, and then to show your kids how to do this by modeling it for them.

Talk about it. Talk about it when you are sitting at home. Talk about how Jesus would handle a situation your kids see on TV. Talk about it when you are going down the road, when you go to bed, and when you get up. Model Jesus, talk about Jesus, *be* about Jesus!

Your kids will become what they see. What are you showing them? Whom are your kids becoming? Are they becoming people who rebuke? Are they becoming lackadaisical, lukewarm Christians? Or are they becoming people-loving, God-fearing, Jesus-following doers of the Word who will bring their kids not just to church but to Jesus Christ?

Also, church: It takes a village to raise a child, doesn't it? We are that village. And while many of you have already raised your children and sent them off to start their own families, that doesn't mean you're finished. A significant number of the kids who come to youth group don't come with their families. These are kids who don't have ideal home situations, who don't have parents who are bringing them to Jesus. Some of these kids have been rebuked! We need to bring these children to Jesus; we need to make time for them like Jesus did. As a church, we need to be the place where kids who have been rebuked can find the outstretched arms of Jesus.

We all have a part to play in this. We all have something to offer. As we move forward with our elementary and early childhood ministry, we're counting on you to step in and find your place in bringing the kids of Erin Church of the Nazarene to Jesus, and to join us in extending the arms of Jesus to the kids of Houston County.

Parents, grandparents, church: it's hard to lead someone to a place you've never been yourself. It's impossible to model the actions of someone you've never spent much time with, or someone you've never met. Jesus is always available to you. He made himself available to you by what he did on the cross. By breaking his body and shedding his blood, he made a way for all those who have been rebuked to find themselves in his arms. Today, church, let us come together and celebrate at the Lord's Table as we remember how he lovingly embraced us so that we can go forth and embrace the world in which we live.

thirteen • TOOLS FOR ENGAGING THE TEXT: DESIRED RESPONSE

■ IT'S PRESUMPTUOUS to think we can fully understand what a biblical writer is thinking unless they tell us—and sometimes they do tell us. We know, for instance, that John's intent in writing his Gospel was evangelistic (John 20:30–31). In reading the letters to the seven churches in Revelation, it becomes clear that their purpose was to encourage faithfulness in the face of suffering, persecution, and the temptation to compromise or grow cold in their faith. Revelation was not meant to strike fear into the hearts of the original readers like some kind of first-century, sci-fi, scare-them-into-submission thriller. Instead, it was meant to encourage the churches to be faithful during a time when faithfulness was anything but easy. Finally, we know that Paul wrote the book of Titus to help a young preacher figure out how to lead in a difficult context. His purpose was not to rebuke Titus but to encourage and equip him.

When we approach a text, another question worth asking is, "What response did the author and the Spirit intend to evoke in the hearts of the hearers? What kind of action, reaction, or response to this text is appropriate?" The assumption behind these questions is that the text will *do* something: Scripture may delight, convict, inspire, challenge, bless, or exhort. It may teach, transform, heal, prod, clarify, or confuse. It may frustrate, encourage, conceal, infuriate, reveal God, misrepresent God, condemn, condone, liberate, or oppress. It may comfort, exalt, restore, or destroy. Or it may provoke any number of unnamed reactions or responses in us.

Sermons do something too—or at least, they should. The question is, what are they doing? And why? And is it true to the text? Preaching must do something, and we must be intentional about defining what that something should be.

Typically there will be several appropriate responses that are true to the text. Take, for example, 1 Samuel 30. David and his band of warriors return to their base camp in Ziklag to discover that that the Amalekites have pillaged the camp, made off with what they could, and burned the rest to the ground. Nothing is left—not even wives or children. This story has a great ending with David and his troops recovering all that was lost, but before it resolves that way, the narrative is rich with possible responses that would be true to the text and offer a variety of approaches for a sermon from this passage. Appropriate responses would include but not be limited to: guarding your house against physical and spiritual attack; developing the kind of relationship with God that stands up to adversity and tragedy; inquiring of God before we act, even when we think we know what to do; treating our enemies well; asking, not assuming; being patient with the weak and exhausted; being willing to fight for the sake of one's family; giving God glory for every victory; not turning on your leaders when you're bitter or looking for someone to blame; being careful, even (or especially) when you think you're standing firm; serving and meeting the needs of others, even when things are going badly in your own life.

For an example from an epistle, let's take a look at Ephesians 4:1–5. Desired responses could include but not be limited to: living a life worthy of our calling; using our gifts for the good of the body; not giving up when unity takes work and it's difficult to stay together; fiercely guarding the unity of the church; being completely humble, gentle, and patient; putting up with each other; putting forth the effort it takes to grow in our knowledge of God; speaking the truth in love; being intentional about our relationships with other believers; serving others; celebrating when we see signs of maturity, growth, and/or Christlikeness; appreciating the giftedness of others rather than competing or comparing. Any preacher would be hard-pressed and ill-advised to include all of these responses, but allowing the Spirit to direct you to one of them when discerning what to say will ensure the sermon is not trying to do something contrary to what the text intends.

Even scriptures that appear on the surface to evoke few—or even a single—desired responses can generate more than meets the eye in an initial reading, if the preacher takes some time to go deeper. For example, Proverbs 22:1–2 says, "A good name is more desirable than great riches; to be esteemed is better than silver or gold. Rich and poor have this in common: The Lord is the Maker of them all." Initially, it seems clear that the desired responses could be: doing whatever it takes to have a good name; valuing reputation over riches; focusing on the universals of our human condition rather than on economic differences. These are all true to the text and would certainly be appropriate.

But a deeper look might lead us to see desired responses like these: taking some time to evaluate our own name and how it is perceived by others; helping a struggling follower of Jesus live up to their new name as a child of God, saint, etc.; being intentional when naming our kids, rather than naming based on popularity; inventorying the names and labels we use to define or describe others as well as those we allow to stick to us; seeing all people as created in the image of God; using the image of God as our measuring stick for the value we place on others; rejecting the world's system of valuing and devaluing human beings and offering them an alternative; building the kind of community and/or church that purposefully levels the playing field on how we value people.

Every response to a text that is consistent with what the author who wrote it and the Spirit who inspired it intend has sermonic possibilities. When we take the time in our process of preparation to explore the ways the text may be calling us to respond, the Spirit may spark an "aha" moment that enables us to proclaim the text in fresh yet faithful ways.

PART 2: WHAT TO SAY

■ ■ ■

Sample Sermon:
Go, Tell Everyone This Great News
Preached by Dwayne Adams

A big part of preparing ourselves to preach is prayerfully discerning what response the text can evoke in the hearers in this particular place, at this particular time. I had the privilege of serving for four years with Dwayne Adams when he was on staff at Clarksville Grace Church of the Nazarene. If you're ever in Florida and want to hear a good sermon, visit Center Pointe Church of the Nazarene in Orlando, where Dwayne is the lead pastor. Dwayne preached this sermon to his congregation at Center Pointe; the purpose of his preaching was to provoke an evangelistic response.

Acts 1:1–8

Today we are going to talk about the very simple yet challenging call of evangelism. And already, with that one word—evangelism—I've lost some of you. So let me pull you back in.

In its verb form, evangelism is simply the act of *announcing, proclaiming,* or *telling.* It's a word we get from the Greek term that means "good news." Good news is something most of us like to share with others. We like to tell people that we got the job; that we got into college; that we're getting married, having a baby, or going on a cruise. We like to share good news with others.

When you walk out of here today, you should have in your hand a very simple, effective, yet stretching tool for sharing the good news of Jesus Christ with others—specifically, with your neighbors. And I don't mean your hypothetical neighbors—I mean the people who live next door, across the street, in the apartment above or below you.

As we enter this Easter season, I believe the central question is, "What do we do now?"

If Jesus is dead and it was all a joke, a lie, or a fairy tale, you go home and get back to life as usual. Back to the hobbies, habits, hurts, hang-ups—the stuff you left behind when you decided to follow Jesus. You go back to the boat and the net you left on the seashore. You go back to the tax booth on the side of the road. You go back to the destructive, abusive relationship. You go back to the things that are killing you and decide to just breathe yourself to death. You accept that this Jesus thing was a nice distraction, but it's time to get back to the real world—the world of every day, where you wake up, go to work, have some fun, go to bed, repeat. Day after day after day. It's like what a college student told me this week: "The meaning of life is simply to survive and reproduce; that's all there is." If Jesus is still dead—if it was all a lie or a prank—then there's no harm done, but let's not waste any more time. Let's eat, drink, and be merry while we still have the chance.

However, if Jesus is alive—if he did rise from the dead as he said he would, and as Scripture says he did—what then? What becomes the purpose, the meaning, the hope of life? Surely it becomes more than surviving and reproducing; more than waking up, going to work, having some fun, going to bed, and repeating *ad nauseam*.

In the book of Acts, Luke makes it clear that Jesus's story didn't end with his resurrection; before ascending into heaven, Jesus told his people what their lives should look like in the new normal. We find his words in a few different places in Scripture; this morning, we're going to focus on Acts 1:1–8.

Jesus suffered, died, was raised to life, and then he presented himself to others, giving them proof that he was alive. Over a period of forty days he appeared to his people and spoke about the kingdom of God.

On one occasion he said to them, "Wait for the promise of the Holy Spirit." He said, "John baptized you, immersed you in water, but now you'll be baptized with the Holy Spirit—immersed in the life and purpose the Holy Spirit has for you."

But his disciples had a question: "After we receive the Holy Spirit, will you then restore the kingdom of Israel? Is this when you'll set things straight once and for all?"

Then, in one of the few instances in Scripture that Jesus directly answers a question, he said, "It is not for you to know the times or dates the Father has set by his own authority" (v. 7). In other words, don't waste your time trying to figure out the future that only God knows. Just know this: "You will receive power when the Holy Spirit comes on you; and you will be my witnesses in Jerusalem, and in all Judea and Samaria, and to the ends of the earth" (v. 8). This is what you are to be concerned with, preoccupied with, and committed to.

So what do we do now? *Go*, and be the witnesses of God in the world. And go in power. Not weak, beaten down, or afraid of what people think—go out in power and tell people about the good news of Jesus Christ. Tell them about freedom from sin, freedom from selfishness. Tell them about real love, joy, hope, and peace. Tell them about the gift of life that Jesus came to bring. What better news could people living in this messed-up, terror-stricken world hear than that of Jesus Christ?

This is the call that Jesus places on all his followers—and it's not optional. While some people have the specific calling of evangelist, *every* Christian has been called to proclaim the hope of Jesus Christ. The choice before us is to evangelize, to grow outward as a church—or to develop hardened, self-centered hearts. As Curtis Hutson writes, "The only alternative to soul-winning is disobedience."[1] That's a disobedience to God's direct call on our lives.

Yet many of us simply don't share the good news. We think it's the preacher's job; the extrovert's job; the college student's job; the new Christian's job; someone else's job. It's been said, and I believe it's true, that the church that doesn't evangelize is living out its final chapter. In calling us to be his witnesses, Jesus is literally asking us to give up our lives for the sake of others.

In the New Testament, the word translated "witness" is the same word also translated as "martyr." It means to give your life up for the sake of another. "You will be my witnesses" means, "You will live and die for the sake of the good news of Jesus Christ."

Here's a summary of evangelism among Protestant believers:

Only 64 percent believe they have a responsibility to share their faith with others.

Only 54 percent say they have shared their faith with someone in the last year.

Only 2 percent say that they share their faith with others on a regular basis.

In other words, the church doesn't seem to be doing very well at fulfilling Jesus's most fundamental call: "Go, be my witnesses." It seems that,

---

1. Curtis Hutson, *Bread for Believers* (Murfreesboro, TN: Sword of the Lord Publishers, 2000), 83.

despite the fact that this is our primary task, when given the opportunity to fulfill it, we don't.

We experienced this dynamic yesterday in our own home. We were all cleaning, preparing for my wife's sister to visit from out of town, when I asked my oldest daughter to clean her room. My actual words were, "I need you to do one thing: go clean your room." Five minutes later, she was straightening up in the living room.

"What are you doing?" I asked.

"I'm straightening this blanket," she said.

"No, baby," I said, "I asked you to go clean your room."

Then I sat down and began to laugh—even from childhood, we're prone to skip *the one thing* we've been asked to do. My daughter was doing a good thing—we needed the blankets to be straightened at some point. But how many times does God look at us and say, "What are you doing?"

We respond, "Oh Jesus, I'm taking care of this stuff. It's good stuff—stuff that needs to be done."

And God says, "But that's not what I asked you to do; please do the one thing I asked you to do."

As believers, the call to *go* tell the good news is *the* fundamental call on our lives. It's simple, and it's clear: share your faith with others. Tell others about Jesus, just as one beggar would tell another where to find bread.

Jesus said, "You will be my witnesses." The first place he names is Jerusalem. Historically, Jerusalem has come to signify the people who live closest to us. Jesus told his apostles to wait in Jerusalem for the Holy Spirit, then to witness *there*, to those who were physically closest to them. There's more to it, but this is where we're going to land today: "Go, be my witnesses in Jerusalem."

When we moved to Orlando, we searched and searched for a house. We were so excited when we finally found one. We couldn't wait to get into the neighborhood, make new friends, have neighbors for our girls to play with, host cookouts.

Before we could move in, we spent about three weeks working on the house. I remember that during those three weeks, I would go out and stand in the driveway looking for people: neighbors, walkers, families with kids. I had this idea that people would just flock to us, their new neighbors, as if we had done them a favor by moving into the neighborhood. But it didn't happen—instead, the place looked like a ghost town.

It's taken a while, but since moving in, we've been able to build some relationships—not nearly to the point we would like, but we know that we're called to go to those who live closest to us. Unfortunately, there are some of us here today who have lived in the same neighborhood for years, yet when it comes to those who live a stone's throw away from us, we don't even know their names—much less their story, or whether they have a relationship with Jesus Christ.

Church, if you are following Christ and you're waiting for people to come to you, you are confused. You—*go!* Be his witnesses. Your Jerusalem includes those God has placed mere steps from your own front door.

With that, I want to issue a simple challenge that involves a tic-tac-toe board. First, draw the board and put your name in the middle. Now fill in the homes or apartments that surround yours. Who are the people who live there? Do you know their names? Do you know their kids, their spouses, their pets?

Here's the challenging part. Start meeting these neighbors by seeking to bless them in some way. Help with yard work, bake them cookies, invite them to a barbecue—you get the idea.

Once you've established a connection, discover ways you can pray for them or their family, and follow up on those requests. Continue to nurture the friendship and ask where they are in their relationship with Jesus. This will help you discover your next steps. Maybe they're a new brother or sister in Christ; maybe they grew up in the church but walked away in college; maybe they want nothing to do with the Jesus or the church. Wherever they are, meet them there, seek to love them, and see them as Jesus sees them—with compassion.

Along the way, share your own story. God's work in your own life is the most powerful tool you have for sharing the gospel. And, as the Spirit leads, invite them into a relationship with Jesus, committing to walk with them on their journey.

fourteen ▪ TOOLS FOR ENGAGING THE TEXT: CONGREGATIONAL BLOCKS

■ **WHEN** we start to get a feel for what the text might be doing in, to, and for the hearer, we can begin to anticipate where the hearers might feel resistance toward the message and the response for which it calls.

It's not just the hearers who experience feelings of resistance—it happens to preachers too. In fact, the best way to anticipate where there might be resistance in the people listening is to recognize areas of resistance in our own spirit. What do we feel reluctant to accept or change? What do we refuse to hear altogether? Whatever it is, there's a good chance that resistance in the pulpit will also be present in the pews.

While it is sometimes dangerous to preach, and preaching does require boldness, we don't go about it like a bull in a china shop. We don't walk into a preaching event ready to ruffle feathers without any consideration for sensitivity toward our audience—at least, not if we want to still be preaching there next week! Alienating people at the outset accomplishes nothing, which is why we should take time to identify where defenses might go up. We do this not to make it easy on ourselves or to water down the message but, rather, to give the truth a chance to work in people's hearts before they resist or dismiss it.

Sometimes the best way to address congregational blocks is to name them, though that isn't always necessary. We do well to employ a variety of strategies not only for identifying blocks but also for helping hearers overcome them. Most of the time, what people need in this process is not information but inspiration. As Walter Brueggemann writes, "The deep places in our lives—places of resistance and embrace—are not ultimately reached by instruction. Those places of resistance and embrace are reached only by stories, by images, metaphors and phrases that line out the world differently, apart from our fear and hurt. The reflection that comes from the poet requires playfulness, imagination, and interpretation."[1]

Congregational blocks can occur even in texts churchgoers might already be very familiar with. Looking at the following sample passages, we can identify a number of questions and concerns that could form congregational blocks:

Mark 10:13–16

What do you mean the whole world didn't revolve around kids back then? What does it mean to receive the kingdom of God like a little child? I'm so old I can't remember what it was like to be a kid. The reference to Jesus touching the children could be a trigger for someone who's been abused. Not everyone has parents who want to bless them or introduce them to Jesus.

John 3:14–21

Who is Nicodemus, and why should I care? What do snakes and Saviors have to do with each other? I've always been taught that my feelings of condemnation come from God because he's angry with me for sinning, but this text says Jesus did not come to condemn, so what am I supposed to believe? What about the fact that I want God to condemn some people for what they've done (rapists, abusers, murderers, the drunk driver who killed someone I know)? How does the conversation between Jesus and Nicodemus end? The text leaves us hanging! Believe? It isn't that easy; I can't believe in something I can't see.

Becoming aware of potential blocks does not guarantee that you, the preacher, will overcome these blocks in every sermon, but failing to even

---

1. Walter Brueggemann, *Finally Comes the Poet: Daring Speech for Proclamation* (Minneapolis: Fortress Press, 1989), 109–10.

recognize their potential will certainly be detrimental to communicating the gospel. The preacher does well to anticipate resistance. This process will take some time. But preparation takes time—and the call to preach is the call to prepare.

Sample Sermon: The Principal's Office
Preached by Nancy Cantrell

Nancy Cantrell pastors Weston Community Church of the Nazarene in Missouri. Nancy says: "When I began prep for this sermon, I had inserted the examples earlier in the structure. Late in the week when I began to practice preaching it, I felt strongly that the examples would become congregational blocks. Initially I removed them completely, but I was nudged by the Holy Spirit that they needed to be there. So I rewrote the sermon, placing the examples at the end instead of the beginning. It worked, and there was a great response to the sermon."

Acts 11:1–18

How many of you have ever been sent to the principal's office?

As a kid, if you get in trouble in the classroom, you might have to go into timeout or stand in the corner (I spent a lot of time in the corner in third grade). If you get in trouble on the playground, you might have to sit on the sidelines or run a lap. If you get in trouble in the cafeteria, you might miss dessert. But being sent to the principal—that's the worst.

Acts 11:1–3 says, "The apostles and the believers throughout Judea heard that the Gentiles also had received the word of God. So when Peter went up to Jerusalem, the circumcised believers criticized him and said, 'You went into the house of uncircumcised men and ate with them.'"

We don't know how much time passes between the events in Acts 10 and the beginning of Acts 11, but it's enough time for the news of Peter's ministry to get back to Jerusalem. Jerusalem isn't that far from Joppa (about thirty miles), but even so, news travels fast. The people who know Peter best (the other *apostles and believers* who are still part of the mother church) receive a report that gentiles—pagans, non-Hebrews—are being included in the community of Christ. We don't know if the believers ask Peter to return to Jerusalem or if he goes back on his own when he gets wind of their reaction. Either way, I think Peter's journey would have felt a whole lot like a trip to the principal's office.

I find it interesting that the believers don't ask Peter about the miracles. In Acts 9, when Peter leaves Jerusalem and heads out to visit the other churches while he's in Lydda, a man named Aeneas, who's been paralyzed and bedridden for eight years, receives the Lord's healing through Peter's ministry. This guy is paralyzed one day and dancing the next—you'd think that would be a topic of conversation.

Then Peter moves on to Joppa, where the disciple Tabitha is dead as a doornail—and the Lord raises her back to life during Peter's prayer. Dead one day, sewing up a storm the next. You'd think the believers would have all sorts of questions about this resurrection!

Acts 9 then tells us that Peter stays a long time in Joppa as a guest of Simon the tanner. If the believers are looking for something to complain about, why not start there? Surely there's a better place for an apostle to stay than with a person who works among dead animals. For a pious Jew, dead things make you unclean, unfit for worship, unfit for ministry. Ceremonial uncleanness aside, there is undoubtedly an odor that clings to anyone who stays in that house. So not only is Peter contaminated according to Jewish law, but now he's also a stinky evangelist. Probably not the best way to draw new people to a church plant.

I think it's wise to take a break here—because we could start to get the picture that these were just some old, crabby church people who were complaining because something new was happening, but that is so far from the truth. These great leaders in Jerusalem are apostles and disciples of Jesus. They are the very people who witnessed Jesus's death, resurrection, and ascension. They're the ones who tarried in the upper room and were filled with the Holy Spirit at Pentecost; who cared for each other, worshiped together, served widows, grew the church, preached the gospel, and healed people. These are *not* mean, backslidden, or hateful people. These apostles and disciples are the people of God—and they're concerned about, even *criticizing* what Peter has been doing. So what is happening here?

Jesus was a Jewish man. He was circumcised, he was educated in the synagogue, and he worshiped in the temple. He participated in the religious events and feasts. Both Matthew and Luke show that Jesus's genealogy is thoroughly connected to the ancestors of the nation of Israel. For these early Christians, following Jesus logically requires being Hebrew; they would never presume to separate the Messiah from Judaism. So when Peter allows gentiles to be included in the church without becoming Jewish, the believers feel he has sacrificed something necessary to salvation. They feel he has compromised what is essential for being a Jesus follower.

When we feel someone is compromising something we hold dear, or something we think is necessary to salvation, we tend to get upset as well. Sometimes when people are very different from us, it's hard to see God working in their lives. When it comes to things we think are nonnegotiable to how we define Christianity, we may find ourselves questioning, even criticizing, those who are doing ministry with unorthodox techniques or among people we believe cannot be included.

In 11:4, Peter begins to tell them the whole story from the beginning. Peter sometimes gets a bad rap for being the run-your-mouth-before-your-brain guy; he's known for jumping in and doing or saying the wrong thing. But here, he gets it right. This is post-Pentecost; the Holy Spirit is indwelling him, teaching him, and leading him. We know he's matured because of what he doesn't do in this text: he doesn't defend himself; he doesn't get mad; he doesn't argue. Peter simply tells the story of how God has worked and how he has obeyed.

In 11:5 he says, "I was in the city of Joppa praying . . ." And Peter is praying so intently that he becomes oblivious to everything around him. The word "trance" here does not refer to mind control or something overtaking Peter's will. Instead, it describes how Peter is totally focused on God, consumed with God, connected with God. And as Peter talks with God, God talks back. Here, he happens to do it in the form of a vision.

Back to 11:5—" . . . and in a trance I saw a vision. I saw something like a large sheet being let down from heaven by its four corners, and it came down to where I was. I looked into it and saw four-footed animals of the earth, wild beasts, reptiles and birds. Then I heard a voice telling me, 'Get up, Peter. Kill and eat.'

"I replied, 'Surely not, Lord! Nothing impure or unclean has ever entered my mouth.'"

For Peter, these food restrictions are very important. He is dedicated to the cause of Christ, which—as he understands it—includes all the Jewish traditions. He is so convinced of the restrictions against unclean food that he argues with a vision from God! The Lord has to repeat the message three times in order to convince Peter to go against something he considers essential to salvation.

"The voice spoke from heaven a second time, 'Do not call anything impure that God has made clean.' This happened three times, and then it was all pulled up to heaven again. Right then three men who had been sent to me from Caesarea stopped at the house where I was staying. The Spirit told me . . ." (vv. 9–11).

Peter is so in tune with the Spirit that when the Spirit asks him to do something against his belief system, against Jewish cultural norms and religious laws, he obeys. But this isn't blind obedience; the Holy Spirit confirms the revelation through others. (Here it is worth noting that some people can have visions or hear voices that may *not* be from the Lord. Any message that is from the Lord will be confirmed by Scripture or by the church.)

Acts 11:12 says, "The Spirit told me to have no hesitation about going with them. These six brothers also went with me, and we entered the man's house." At the time, Peter may not have realized why the Lord was sending all these people to him, but God knew what he was doing: in Jewish legal cases, you needed seven witnesses to verify an event. God was helping the early church change their perspective, and in the process, he provided the perfect number of witnesses needed to satisfy the law. God still provides what we need today when he calls us to change.

Acts 11:13–16 continues, "He told us how he had seen an angel appear in his house and say, 'Send to Joppa for Simon who is called Peter. He will bring you a message through which you and all your household will be saved.' As I began to speak, the Holy Spirit came on them as he had come on us at the beginning. Then I remembered what the Lord had said: 'John baptized with water, but you will be baptized with the Holy Spirit.'"

This wasn't something Peter dreamed up. It wasn't a strategy to increase membership at the First Church of Joppa or to benefit himself in some way. Peter prayed until he was united with the Holy Spirit, he followed the Holy Spirit, and he obeyed the Holy Spirit. And when he did, the Holy Spirit changed lives, the church, and the world. We are Christians today because the Holy Spirit (not Peter) moved to include gentiles.

"So if God gave them the same gift he gave us who believed in the Lord Jesus Christ, who was I to think that I could stand in God's way?" (v. 17). Here Peter is saying, "I felt just like you do about Judaism being essential to discipleship, but God showed me a different way. There's no way I'm getting in the way of his will or his work." We too need to be sure that we are in tune with and connected to what the Holy Spirit is doing. But sometimes it's really hard.

Engage magazine tells the story of how Euless First Church of the Nazarene in Euless, Texas, became involved in a unique outreach ministry. In a June 2012 article, pastor Zack Smithson spoke to *Engage* about how they got started:

> [Carole] Lafreniere is a sex industry survivor who now helps women and children escape the sex trade. She has established a ministry to strip club employees by going into clubs and washing dancers' feet, giving them pedicures and, according to Zack, "loving on them in the name of Jesus."
>
> After [Zack told] his wife, Corrie, about his meeting with Lafreniere, Corrie was on board.
>
> Lafreniere gave Corrie an avenue of what to do and where to go. In November 2010, she accompanied Lafreniere to a club just a few miles from Zack and Corrie's church. [. . . .]
>
> Lafreniere accompanied Corrie to the club for the first few months, but gradually handed over responsibility until Corrie and a small group of women from the Euless First Church of the Nazarene were handling the outreach themselves.
>
> The group goes in one Saturday a month at noon to minister to the women working that afternoon by washing their feet and giving them pedicures. The number of women working ranges from three to twelve, depending on the day. After doing this for a few months, the church group also realized that the dancers were hungry. Now they bring a potluck dinner, too. [. . . .]
>
> Corrie says that the goal of the ministry is to show the dancers the love of Christ. "If they ask questions [about who we are], we answer, but we talk to them about their lives. We don't want them to feel judged. We want them to feel loved and respected."
>
> That message must be getting across. One Saturday, a dancer looked at Corrie and said, "You guys must really love us."[2]

This next excerpt is from the website of Trinity Family Midtown Church of the Nazarene in Kansas City, Missouri:

---

2. Mandie Schaper, "Texas Church Ministering to Strip Club Dancers," Engage (June 19, 2012), http://engagemagazine.com/content/texas-church-ministering-strip-club-dancers.

Sample Sermon: Nancy Cantrell

Love Wins: LGBT was founded in 2009 as a ministry of Trinity Family Midtown Church of the Nazarene located in the heart of Kansas City, MO. This ministry exists to build bridges between the church and the LGBT community. This congregation holds deeply the belief that God loves those with a different sexual orientation and the Church of the Nazarene should too. Pastors Andy and Sarah McGee along with their congregation believe that God's love is active and that he intends for his people to share his love with everyone. So they do the slow, long-term, tedious work of believing in the power of God to help people get to know him. Years of patiently loving, caring, and teaching without judgment.[3]

And this is from the Church of the Nazarene's magazine *Holiness Today*:

Because of threats and acts of terror happening around the world, it is not uncommon to hear some Christians speak against immigration. Some strongly oppose accepting refugees, believing that terrorists might be infiltrating programs to receive the migrants.

The Church of the Nazarene in the Middle East offers a powerful example of outreach and compassion as an alternative to fear and risk-aversion. Our churches in Jordan and Lebanon have a unique position as their countries are absorbing approximately 1,400,000 and 2,372,000 refugees respectively. Nazarenes are welcoming and serving the refugees that are fleeing from Syria and Iraq. The churches are providing food, blankets and clothing, and conducting special church services which are full with many who are from non-Christian backgrounds. The Nazarene schools are also providing educational opportunities for the children.

When asked if they are afraid that terrorists might be in the groups that come, the pastors respond that they don't even consider that. All they know is that the people are hungry, possessing only the clothes on their backs, and have broken lives.

It is amazing to see the desire to serve but also the respect shown to those who are so different from them. They believe that God is bringing people to them to find new life through his grace.

---

3. https://trinityfamilyonline.org.

Immigrants and refugees are moving all over the world. It is important that Christians and Nazarenes ask, "Are we as hospitable and open to these new neighbors?"[4]

If we're honest, some of us would have difficulty participating in ministries like these. We would have difficulty not casting judgment and allowing God to make changes in God's time. It can be difficult to befriend, love, or even eat with people who are very unlike us—sounds a little like Acts 11. When Peter finished telling the story of how God had begun to move, the brethren in Jerusalem reevaluated their own beliefs, attitudes, and actions. Acts 11:18 says, "When they heard this, they had no further objections and praised God, saying, 'So then, even to Gentiles God has granted repentance that leads to life.'"

Our resurrected Lord is all about life. He has given salvation, redemption, and life to you and me. He extends life to the broken, the hurting, the dead. He extends life to those who don't act, think, or behave like we do. Jesus is working by and through us as we pray and obey his voice, his leading, and his Word. Weston, Missouri, and the surrounding areas need us. They need us to be on the streets, in homes, in businesses. They need us to befriend, love, and eat with people who may be nothing like us. Are we ready to put aside our objections, concerns, even criticisms, and choose to praise God? I hope, pray, and dream that, together, we can become an Acts 11 church and reach anyone and everyone with God's amazing, awesome grace.

---

4. Lindell Browning, "Immigrants, Refugees, or Angels," *Holiness Today,* March/April 2016, holinesstoday.org/immigrants.

fifteen ▪ TOOLS FOR ENGAGING THE TEXT: ENGAGING THE SENSES

▪ SENSORY questions may not provide direction for the sermon, but they do help the preacher engage the text more fully and imaginatively. The goal of engaging the senses is not so much to find sermonic direction as to deepen the preacher's engagement with the text. Why does this matter? Because the more we get into the text, the more the text can get into us. To some this may seem like an unnecessary step, especially because it takes yet more time. But, as we have been saying all along, the call to preach is the call to prepare, and preparation takes time.

One of the exercises I do with my students is to have them write a description of the inside of their car. It's great fun—we learn who's messy, who's a neat freak, who has kids, who eats in their car, who pays attention to detail, and who doesn't. When done well, these descriptions can put the rest of the class right there inside the car: we can smell yesterday's French fries; feel the sand on the floorboards under our feet; hear the crackling of the AM radio because the FM doesn't work; taste the dust as the door slams shut; feel the stuffiness caused by the broken AC.

Why is this important? Because if you can put me in your car, you can put me in the text. If you can engage my senses in a description of the temple, of Achan's tent, of the upper room, or of Jesus's tomb, then you create a moment in which I can find myself in the story. And if I find myself in the story, I want to know what happens in the story. If I can see God moving or acting in the story, I might just desire for God to move or act in my own life.

If I can relate, I'm in. And one of the best ways to get me to relate is to appeal to my senses. The smell of a spring rain gets to me; so does the smell of a wet dog, the touch of a callused hand, or the sound of a baby's cry. The sight of blood affects me; the feeling of tension from knotted shoulders or trembling fear are familiar to me. Engage those details, and you've engaged me—because sense appeal begets identification. If I can identify, I'll listen; if I listen, there is opportunity for the Word to transform me. Sense appeal helps transformation happen.

To varying degrees, the biblical writers appeal to and engage the senses with the particular details they provide. These details serve a purpose greater than description; their purpose is connection. We've all felt the ominous stillness before the storm or the threatening wind during it. We've all seen or met someone who was born disabled. We've all heard a crowd shout in unison. We've all smelled smoke from a fire.

The question for preachers is this: What do we hear, see, taste, touch, or smell in a given text? Experiencing a text with our senses can lead us to experience the God of the text and the transformation God wants to work in us.

Listening and reading can teach us a lot about using description to engage the senses. Some of the most skilled, sensory-rich wordsmiths are play-by-play radio sports broadcasters. Listening to a game on the radio is a lot different than watching it on television. Even if you are not a sports enthusiast, try it sometime. The next time you're driving, turn on the radio, find a ball game, and listen to the way the commentator recounts what's happening. The good ones are always describing which way the wind is blowing the stadium flags; the color of the jerseys the team is wearing; the look on the player's face as she grimaces after spraining an ankle. Good commentators help us hear the roars of disgust at the referee who made a bad call. They help us see the celebration in the end zone. Pick a sport you don't know much about and see what you can envision as the commentator creates word pictures of the events. These aren't just tools of the trade for sports broadcasters—they're also skills that can serve a preacher well when developed with practice.

Another great source of sensory-rich language is found in print. Certain writers, including poets and those who write for outdoor magazines, are great at using words to paint pictures and draw you into the scene they're describing.

I'm sure you see the significance. Developing skills in sensory-rich description doesn't just make a story more interesting or a scene more compelling. It opens the hearer to participation, to identification. Put them in the car. Put them in the scene. Put them in the text, and the text can find its way into them.

If you preach every week, then you're probably working on a sermon right now (and hopefully it's working on you too). Give this a try with the text you're already engaging: what do you see, hear, taste, touch, or smell as you walk around in the text? How might asking sensory questions enliven not only your engagement with the text but also the sermon that emerges from it?

sixteen ▪ TOOLS FOR ENGAGING THE TEXT: POSSIBLE DIRECTIONS

I think good preachers should be like bad kids. They ought to be naughty enough to tiptoe up on dozing congregations, steal their bottles of religion pills, spirituality pills, and morality pills, and flush them all down the drain. The church, by and large, has drugged itself into thinking that proper human behavior is the key to its relationship with God. What preachers need to do is force it to go cold turkey with nothing but the word of the cross—and then be brave enough to stick around while it goes through the inevitable withdrawal symptoms. But preachers can't be that naughty or brave unless they're free of their own need for the dope of acceptance. And they won't be free of their need until they can trust the God who has already accepted them, in advance and dead as doornails, in Jesus. Ergo, the absolute indispensability of trust in Jesus' Passion: unless the faith of preachers is in that alone—and not in any other person, ecclesiastical institution, theological system, moral prescription, or master recipe for human loveliness— they will be of very little use in the pulpit.
—Robert Farrar Capon[1]

■ BY THE time we have walked around in the text, made observations, asked questions, and maybe even heard a few answers, it becomes obvious that there's no way we can include everything we've thought or learned in one sermon. Throughout your process of preparation, you've likely had

---

1. Capon, *The Foolishness of Preaching*, 14.

different ideas about the directions the sermon could go, and now it's time to write those ideas down.

Ideas for possible direction can come at any point, from any of the questions we use to engage the text. Many a sermon has stemmed from the image of God revealed in the text. Others have flowed from the good news in the text, the tension that can't be ignored by a congregational block, or the insight that comes from a perspective we never considered. Occasionally the sermonic spark happens in the first reading and initial observations.

When it comes to possible directions, I encourage you to write down *all* your ideas—even those that initially appear to be headed down the wrong track. Pray over them. Which one resonates with you? Which one haven't you addressed in a while (or ever)? Which direction would God have you go with this text, at this time, for these people?

Let's look at potential sermon directions in the sample passages below.

Matthew 25:14–30

The parable of the talents has several possible sermonic directions.

God Will Never Give Us More Than We Can Handle

Examine this platitude's frequent misapplication to trials, trouble, and suffering, and contrast it with the text, which shows God will not give us more *talents or resources* than we can handle. Discuss how this should motivate us to handle (or steward) our talents and resources well. Stewardship of all resources (not just money) could be the focus and direction of the sermon.

Great Expectations

Focus on the ways God trusts and entrusts us. We could use other scriptures as examples: God trusted his creation to Adam and Eve, trusted his message to the prophets, and trusted his mission to the church.

Return on Investment

Use the economic metaphor to explore how we invest in relationships and with our resources. Discuss the dividends of kingdom living.

Taking Risks

Focus on how we must be willing to take risks rather than playing it safe to protect ourselves. Following Jesus is a life of faith and of risk, not a sedentary life of self-protection or self-preservation. What risky things do we need to attempt as individuals? As a community?

The Best Defense Is a Good Offense

This text calls for an active faith, a purposeful living-out of the gospel through maximizing what we've been given. This is a faith of "dos," not "don'ts." This sermon could focus on faith as practice rather than faith as restriction.

The Master's Absence

In the parable, the master's absence is a sign of trust, not abandonment. In the same way, the sermon could emphasize how the seeming absence of God signifies not distance but God's trust that we will be about his business as we await his return.

Ezekiel 34:11–16, 20–24

This text comes up in the Lectionary for Christ the King Sunday. Here are some of the many and varied sermonic possibilities.

Be Careful Whom You Trust

Both then and now, the kings and shepherds who offer rescue tend to promise more than they deliver. We look to the wrong places for rescue all the time: to a loan shark for financial rescue; to an unhealthy relationship or an ungodly but available person for rescue from loneliness; to politicians for rescue from inferiority; to celebrities for rescue from insignificance. Misplaced trust always leads to the same place: exile. Judah found that out the hard way, but even though they looked to kings for rescue, God the Rescuer came searching for them. In the sermon, you could paint several pictures of exile (personal, familial, national), and then go to the text. Just as God provides a way out of exile for Judah, God also provides a way out of exile for us.

Don't Blame Me! I Voted for . . .

In our highly charged political climate, people are quick to assign blame, typically to someone (anyone!) other than themselves. In Ezekiel, everyone is at fault for the sad state of affairs. The king and other leaders (the shepherds) are at fault for exploiting the people who trusted them. But the sheep are at fault for imitating their kings by exploiting one another, and for expecting kings to do what only God can do (remember, the sheep cast their vote for the crooked shepherds to begin with). The text describes how God comes to them as the true Shepherd, King, Rescuer, and Healer. He votes for us, no matter how we voted in previous elections or where it landed us.

How Did We Get Here?

How did we get into the situation we're facing? How are we getting out? God gives the answer to both of these questions. Sometimes we say, "It doesn't matter how we got here; it is what it is." But there is almost always value in figuring out how we got here—especially when here isn't where we want to be. This is true for nations, marriages, families, finances, addiction, and more. Until we understand how we got here (and how we individually contributed to getting here), we're more likely to end up back in the same spot—even after we've been rescued from it. So we also need to ask, "How will we keep from going back?" The text is explicit about how Judah got into exile and how they will get out (God will rescue them). Implied but not explicit in the text is that they can keep from going back to exile by trusting in the Shepherd whom God provides rather than trusting in their corrupt rulers.

The Biggest Loser

Judah's kings and leaders (shepherds) were losers. Judah's fat sheep were losers. And Judah's exploited were losing all the way around—they probably felt like they just couldn't win no matter what they did. In that place of need and vulnerability, God came to them. God came to the rescue of losers—and he still does.

Animal Farm

Our worldly leaders often buy into systems of oppression and become drunk with power. As Christians, our leadership is different—it's founded on the call to follow the Good Shepherd. When we use the gospel to comfort and serve ourselves at the expense of our neighbors, we have missed the point. The people around us deserve God's blessings as much as we do.

A few other questions I ask on occasion during sermon prep and which you might also want to consider asking: What will be different (specifically) if this sermon is received and lived out well? What kind of person does this text aim to form? What kind of community is formed if this text is lived? How can/does/should a sermon from this text equip God's people?

A brief word here about the balance between sermons aimed at individuals and sermons expressly intended to form and shape a community collectively: While personal piety is important, the Scriptures rarely address individuals. The typical context is corporate, communal. The Old Testament is written to, for, and about the community called Israel; the New Testament is written to, for, and about the community called the church. It is important to call for individual response in our preaching, but the corporate nature of the faith requires us to constantly consider the kind of community that will be formed by any given text. In our culture of consumeristic Christianity, there is a great need for preaching that helps form not only individuals but also communities of faith. If ever there was a need for a community to stand out, to give an alternative picture of relationships and reality, that need is now. And if our preaching is to help form this kind of community, we must be attentive to the corporate implications of every text from which we preach.

Seventeen • SERMON PURPOSE

■ AT SOME point in the preparation process, there has to be an "aha" moment about what to say. When the Spirit finally reveals it to us, we experience relief, clarity, and an immediate desire to discern how best to articulate the word we've been given. Between the "aha" of what to say and the "aha" of how to say it, the purpose of the sermon should be clearly stated. Bryan Chapell says it like this: "Once you've researched the passage but before you start writing your sermon, you need to know what you're going to tell people to do, so you have a target and you know how to form the message of your sermon."[1]

Beginning with the end in mind is a habit of highly successful people—and for preachers, it's a *must*. If we don't know where we are going or how we plan to get there, the sermon will leave the hearers with a sense that they've traveled without knowing where or why. Whether preaching from a fully written manuscript, a few notes, a general outline, or no helps at all, the establishment of the sermon purpose is essential. Without it, the sermon will lack direction and coherence, no matter how intelligent or inspired the preacher. Thomas Long describes "focus" and "function" statements that help give the preacher clarity:

---

1. Bryan Chapell, "Application without Moralism" in *The Art & Craft of Biblical Preaching: A Comprehensive Resource for Today's Communicators*, ed. Haddon Robinson and Craig Brian Larson (Grand Rapids: Christianity Today International, 2005), 292.

A focus statement is a concise description of the central, controlling, and unifying theme of the sermon. In short, this is what the whole sermon will be "about."

Example for a sermon from Romans 8:28–39: "Because we have seen in Jesus Christ that God is for us, we can be confident that God loves and cares for us even when our experience seems to deny it."

A function statement is a description of what the preacher hopes the sermon will create or cause to happen for the hearers.

Example for sermon from Romans 8:28–39: To reassure and give hope to troubled hearers in the midst of, not apart from, their distress.[2]

Sermon *content* is defined by the focus statement; sermon *purpose* is defined by the function statement. While Long suggests using two separate statements to define sermon content and purpose, Frank Thomas recommends using one sermon purpose statement that says, "I propose to . . . to the end that the hearer will . . ."[3]

After "propose to," the preacher should list a verb: I propose to [show, teach, evoke, admonish, rebuke, correct, inspire, explain, etc.]. The language should be precise, succinct, and consistent with the purpose of the text. What were Jeremiah, Paul, or John trying to accomplish with the scriptures they wrote? The sermon should seek to accomplish the same thing. The second part of the sermon purpose statement requires another verb that represents the specific response we're aiming for: I propose to . . . to the end that the hearer will [confess, believe, repent, reconcile a relationship, trust God with their finances, build relationships with nonbelievers, spend time in the Word every day, get involved in a ministry of the church, pray for their city, serve their spouse, lead their children, share their story, etc.].

The more precise the purpose statement, the more clarity we'll have as we write, outline, and organize the sermon. Knowing where God

---

2. Long, *The Witness of Preaching*, 86.

3. Frank Anthony Thomas, *They Like to Never Quit Praisin' God: The Role of Celebration in Preaching* (Cleveland: Pilgrim Press, 2013).

wants to take us is crucial in the preparation process. Only after we have a clear sense of the Spirit's direction are we ready to explore the variety of routes (i.e., sermon forms) to get there.

But if we already have an idea of where we're going with the sermon, is it really necessary to take the time to articulate and perfect a sermon purpose statement? Personally, I have found that a specific plan is better than a general direction. A little more time on the front end to clarify content and purpose generally saves time on the back end of sermon development. Sermon purpose statements are a great discipline even for seasoned preachers. The sharper the focus and the clearer the purpose, the higher the likelihood of sermon impact.

One biblical example of a purpose statement comes from the Gospel of John. Near the end of John's account, he states his purpose: "Jesus performed many other signs in the presence of his disciples, which are not recorded in this book. But these are written that you may believe that Jesus is the Messiah, the Son of God, and that by believing you may have life in his name" (20:30–31). We know from John's statement that he uses miracles (or signs, as he calls them) as the means to an end—the end being the salvation of the reader. This statement is clear, concise, and intentional. Our sermons should have the same clarity of purpose. In the process of sermon preparation, there will always be more examples, stories, thoughts, and points that never find their way into the sermon. The sermon purpose statement helps assure that everything in the sermon serves to accomplish its purpose.[4]

---

4. "Every sermon issues from the text in what Haddon Robinson calls 'the Big Idea.' The big idea is the thesis. It is a short statement that expresses what you're going to talk about and what the sermon will call the reader to do about it. Almost all homileticians call for this approach." Calvin Miller, *Preaching: The Art of Narrative Exposition* (Grand Rapids: Baker Books, 2006), 105.

eighteen ▪ CONSULTING THE SCHOLARS

Prayer and humility before the text do not guarantee exegetical success.
—N. T. Wright[1]

■ I HAVE intentionally held off on a discussion of consulting the scholars until now because I do not want them to confuse or interfere with the process of exploring the text on the text's terms. Scholars are wonderful resources, but they cannot replace the work of prayerfully seeking the Spirit, whose voice we most need to hear. As Calvin Miller reminds us, "Listeners are needy and want a firsthand confessional exegesis of the text. They want to see inside the preacher's soul. They want to know how the preacher first discovered the text, how it came to mean so much, and in what ways it is found to be true. This depth-of-soul exegesis makes or breaks a sermon."[2]

However, to preach without doing the due diligence of exegetical study is a gross neglect of the call. The call to preach is the call to prepare. We need to ensure that our ideas are theologically sound, exegetically accurate, and aligned with the history of interpretation. Therefore,

---

1. N. T. Wright, "New Perspectives on Paul (2003)" in *Pauline Perspectives: Essays on Paul, 1978–2013* (Minneapolis: Fortress Press, 2013), 277.
2. Calvin Miller, *Preaching: The Art of Narrative Exposition* (Grand Rapids: Baker Books, 2006), 125.

I recommend consulting the scholars to see if they can 1) confirm or 2) correct the direction of the sermon.

What happens if the scholars assert that the direction you wanted to go is heretical, inaccurate, or inconsistent with the contextual claims of the text? Has all that time spent with the text been wasted? Wouldn't it have been better to consult the scholars first to save the trouble and frustration of going down the wrong road? Absolutely not! If you as a preacher have asked all the questions recommended in this book and have prayed, sought, studied, and meditated only to arrive at a wrong conclusion, then chances are the same thing has happened (and will happen) to your hearers. Maybe your trip down the wrong road has been informed by folk theology or misguided insights, which can set the stage for your sermon to correct a widely held misconception of a text. None of our engagement with the text or with the God of the text is ever in vain. God can and will make the most of our time and effort; he will redeem them for his glory, our good, and the good and growth of our hearers.

Proverbs 19:2 says, "Desire without knowledge is not good—how much more will hasty feet miss the way!" Waiting to consult the scholars also gives us the time and space to figure out what questions we want to ask. We don't go to the scholars to determine which questions to ask; we go to them for answers to the questions we've raised in our own engagement with the text. And we don't go to the scholars to decide what to preach; we go to them to correct or confirm the word that has already begun to burn within us.

Stephen Farris describes the difference between a scholarly and a homiletical approach this way:

> The distinction between sermon and exegetical lecture is . . . real. An exegetical lecture is essentially descriptive. It explains the text by speaking intelligently, one hopes, about the text. For the most part, methods identical to or at least similar to those of the historian, the literary scholar, or the social anthropologist are used to explicate the text. The hope of the lecturer is that the listener will understand the text more profoundly as a result. With respect to the text, the

lecturer hopes to uncover *meaning*. With respect to the listener, *understanding* is the aim of the lecturer.

The preacher, on the other hand, prays that the sermon may become an encounter between the congregation and the living God. The aim of the preacher is not primarily to uncover meaning or to create understanding, but to hear and speak a word from God. In this encounter what may be communicated is not information about God but something of God's own self. The goal of the sermon is therefore not meaning as such, but *revelation*. The sermon can be, amazingly enough, a part of the process of revelation.

This insight makes one aware that the task of preaching is indeed different from the task of eliciting meaning from a text. Meaning can, in principle, be found in or created from any text and the process of discovering meaning can be described, and in academic work usually is described, without any reference to God whatsoever. Revelation, on the other hand, cannot occur without the presence and activity of God. The word "revelation" contains within its definition in theology some sense of the self-disclosing activity of God. The concept of revelation is meaningless without a doctrine of the presence and work of God.[3]

In the section below, I'd like to draw upon the work of those who have written, taught, conversed, and commiserated with me about preaching, and offer some suggestions about approaching exegetical work from a preacher's perspective.

Guidelines for Using Exegesis in Preaching

Preparation

1. What do I need to know about the historical, social, or political context to avoid misinterpreting the text? Understanding context should prevent us from misrepresenting the text to mean something it could never have meant at the time it was written—for example, historical context is key when working with prophetic and apocalyptic passages.

---

3. Farris, *Preaching That Matters,* 11.

We have to keep asking the question, "What did this mean to the original hearers?" Knowing the context does not mean we have to teach the congregation the context in excruciating detail. It does mean, however, that our sermons will be adequately informed by the context so that we do not make the text say something in our context that it was never intended to say in the original context. The goal is to stay true to the intent, claims, and truth of the text.

2. What do I need to know about the biblical context to avoid misinterpreting the text? We can see one example of this in Romans 8:28–29. "God works all things together for the good . . . " is often quoted to console people experiencing hardship—anyone, from the person who's had a bad day with a flat tire and a parking ticket, to someone who has experienced real trauma. When taken in its proper context, however, the "good" of 8:28 is defined in 8:29—and failing to account for this can result in a mishandling of the text. What is the good? It is the fact that God will work in and through all things to conform the people who love him into the image of his Son, Jesus. The good is ultimately Christlikeness. This is not just a comforting word; it is a challenging and hopeful word that's much bigger than a Band-Aid on a bad day. For another example, allegorical interpretation works with the parable of the sower because this is how Jesus intends it to be interpreted. The different soils correspond to different conditions of the heart. However, allegorical interpretation does not work with historical narratives like the healing of the lepers in Luke 17. To ignore the clues provided *by* the biblical context itself is to open oneself to a mishandling of the text.

The biblical context is what reconciles the seeming contradiction between writers James (faith without works is dead in James 2:26) and Paul (saved by grace, not works, in Ephesians 2). Prooftexting (or "concordance preaching," as I call it) often results in misinterpretation because it fails to consider the larger context within which texts are located. James and Paul were speaking to different audiences who were struggling with different shortcomings in their understanding and practice of the faith. Paul's audience put too much stock in works; James's audience didn't put enough. It is critical that we locate the pericope in the context of the chapter, book, and biblical/theological whole to correctly divide the word of truth.

3. How does the original language unlock the text in ways English cannot? A language barrier isn't just something that exists between people speaking different tongues—the Bible itself can be a language barrier. The images, phrases, and vocabulary of the text can act as a barrier to modern readers and hearers. Just as it takes work to understand the terminology of a different professional field (the medical field, for example), it often takes some work to discern the meaning of a theological text like the Bible. This barrier can be compounded by the fact that the Bible wasn't written in our native language to begin with—the underlying images, nuances, and connotations behind an ancient Hebrew or Greek word aren't as obvious to the English, Spanish, German, Korean, French, Russian, or even contemporary Greek reader.

For example, we don't immediately see, in the description of the untamed tongue in James 3, that the word translated "untamed" is used only one other place in Scripture: the description of the demon-possessed man in Mark 5. A little exegetical work expands already rich images and opens up the text so we can better understand its significance. This often makes the text more accessible, understandable, and applicable.

We see the benefit of exegetical work when it comes to words that mean something different in Scripture than they do in our current context or culture. For example, in Matthew's account of the Sermon on the Mount, Jesus says, "Be perfect, therefore, as your heavenly Father is perfect" (Matthew 5:48). In English, the term "perfect" is associated with flawlessness and performance. However, the Greek word from which we get that translation—*teleios*—has more to do with purpose than performance. Jesus is exhorting the crowd (and us) to live into the purpose for which God made them. The call is not to do so without mistakes or flaws in our performance but to operate from an awareness of and commitment to our God-created purpose. This is just one example of how the original languages can help us understand a text in ways we otherwise couldn't.

4. How do the scholars confirm or correct my previous assumptions and experiences with the text? This question prevents us from over-

riding the text's meaning with our own ignorance or misperceptions.[4] Sometimes we find corrections to our interpretations; sometimes we will argue with the scholars; and sometimes we will find that we need to make significant changes because our insights, even though sincere, are off base somehow.

Proclamation

1. When possible, present exegetical information in the form of narrative description. Don't just teach it, describe it; don't just tell it, show it. When preaching on the healing of the man with abnormal swelling (sometimes translated "dropsy") in Luke 14:1–6, don't give a technical definition of dropsy; *describe* it so your hearers can visualize the man and his suffering. This is one of the best uses of exegetical material: incorporate it into vivid descriptions to engage the senses.

The same principle applies when talking about places: When referring to Ephesus, don't just say, "Ephesus was a city with many shrines to other gods." Instead, paint a picture by walking us through a street in this bustling city. Guide us past the shrines and show us the prostitutes at the temple. Show, don't tell.

2. Don't introduce new exegetical material at the end of the sermon. Typically, when you're seeking to end a sermon by eliciting a response in the hearer's heart, presenting new cognitive material does not help—appealing to the intellect does not typically inspire emotive response. Our aim at the end of the sermon is not the head but the heart.

I'm not suggesting we exclude cognitive material from the sermon; I'm saying that where we place it in our structure can either help or hinder the emotive process that encourages response. This is not manipulation. It is an awareness of the emotive process and how to use it to maximize the gospel's impact on the hearer so that it might touch, inspire, and transform both heart and mind.

3. Be selective with insights gained from word study. Don't turn the sermon into a lecture on Greek or Hebrew. Instead, simply share an

---

4. Here I use "ignorance" to refer not to intellectual deficiency, but to its original definition of limited knowledge.

insight and move on. Why? For one thing, a sermon is not meant to be a lecture. For another, too much emphasis on Greek or Hebrew can cause congregants to question whether it's even worth it for them to read the Bible on their own if they aren't literate in the original languages. Information from word study needs to be used sparingly but proficiently, always with the intent of revealing the depth and beauty of the text (rather than the intellect of the preacher).

4. Use the sermon purpose statement as a filter for sermon content. Not every Greek word or insight about historical or textual context needs to be preached; solid exegetical work can inform a sermon without appearing in the sermon manuscript. Only include details that are crucial for bringing about the intended response. Here I am referring to exegetical insights, but the same could be said of any other material in the sermon.

I liken a great sermon to a great glass of sweet tea. For several years I lived in the South, where every restaurant serves sweet tea. Too much water makes the tea too weak; too many teabags makes it too strong. The ratio must be right. Sermons are very much the same. Too much water (images or illustrations) can weaken the sermon. Too many teabags (exegetical material) can make it too strong, causing the text to seem more bitter than sweet. The right mixture makes for the best tea—and the best sermons.

PART 2: WHAT TO SAY

■ ■ ■
Sample Sermon: *Sozo*
Preached by Steve Estep

From time to time, exegetical work will not only confirm or correct but will also hold the key to an "aha" moment. That's what happened in this sermon. A deeper look at a word often translated as "saved" or "salvation" yielded an exegetical insight that the Spirit used to ignite a sermonic spark.

Acts 4:5–12

Last week we took a trip to the temple in Jerusalem with Peter and John, who were going to pray. On the way in we met a disabled man. We don't know his name, background, family situation, or anything more than that he was in his forties, had been disabled from birth, and was dropped at the gate called Beautiful, where he begged for money. But when Peter and John came by, God provided him something much better than spare change. In the power of the Spirit, Peter said to him, "Silver or gold I do not have, but what I do have I give you. In the name of Jesus Christ of Nazareth, walk" (3:6). Peter reached out, took him by the right hand, and lifted him up. In an instant his feet and ankles were made strong, and he started jumping around and praising God. Forty years of disabled existence was transformed in an instant by the name of Jesus.

A crowd quickly formed, and Peter seized the opportunity to tell them about Jesus. He shot straight with them: "*You are guilty of rejecting Jesus. You are responsible for the death of the Author of life.*" As Peter spoke, the Spirit brought conviction, and the crowd was brought face to face with their own sin. Even though they had acted in ignorance (which we've all done), God was merciful and, in his great grace, was giving them an opportunity to turn their lives around—the biblical word is "repent."

That's where we stopped the story last week. Several people here responded like the many who believed in Acts: they accepted God's invitation to repent and had their sins forgiven and their souls refreshed. Today, we continue the story.

When the crowd formed around Peter, John, and the formerly disabled man who was jumping around praising God, the temple bosses were quick to get over there, ready to disperse the crowd if there was anything out of order. These controllers of the temple courts didn't like it when Peter started talking about Jesus's resurrection, so they quickly had Peter and John arrested. The last time that happened, the person they arrested had been crucified, so it's hard to tell what Peter and John might have been feeling at that moment. Whatever they were feeling, they were ready by the next day when they were brought before the rulers, elders, and teachers of the law to be interrogated. This is where we pick up the story.

The leaders' question was simple: "By what power or what name did you do this?" (4:7).

Then Peter, filled with the Holy Spirit, said, "It is by the name of Jesus Christ of Nazareth, whom you crucified but whom God raised from the dead, that this man stands before you healed . . . Salvation is found in no one else, for there is no other name under heaven given to mankind by which we must be saved" (vv. 10, 12).

Peter's message to the authorities is the same as his message to the crowds the day before: Jesus. You crucified him. God raised him. He's the one who made this man well, and his is the only name that can do that.

There is no other name by which we must be saved. The word "saved" in 4:12 comes from the Greek word *sozo*, which literally means "to heal, make well, restore to health." It also means "to preserve one who is in danger of destruction—to rescue, save, or deliver."[5] To say the lame man was saved is to say he was healed, restored, made well. It's a broader term than we may envision when we hear the phrase "Jesus saves." When Peter says, "Salvation is found in no one else . . . " the word "salvation" includes the idea of being saved from destruction or hell, but it also connotes being healed, made whole, restored. We could say a car that has been restored: *sozo*. A broken leg healed: *sozo*. A broken heart comforted: *sozo*. A person delivered from floodwaters just before their car is swept away: *sozo*. It's an image-rich word.

When Peter and John declared the power of Jesus's name to save, the authorities couldn't argue because the evidence was standing right in front of them—a man restored in body. I think we can also infer that he was restored in spirit by believing in Jesus, in whose name he had been healed.

---

5. Bible Study Tools, s.v. "Sozo," https://www.biblestudytools.com/lexicons/greek/nas/sozo.html.

This growing community of the resurrected was evidence of the healing, wholeness, and restoration that can only be found in Jesus. John Holbert writes, "the Hebrew *shalom* . . . in part underlies the Greek term salvation. The Hebrew means, at the base, 'wholeness' or 'unity' or 'oneness.' What salvation in Jesus promises is a fresh wholeness, a divine unity whereby a broken world can be restored."[6]

We don't know what the lame man looked like, but I think I saw him last Sunday. He looked like a young husband, father, and soldier in the 160th Special Operations Aviation Regiment (SOAR) who responded to God's invitation to repentance last week. He told me later that he knew he'd been forgiven. We'd call that *sozo* in Jesus's name.

We don't know what the lame man looked like, but I think I saw him on Tuesday. I saw evidence of the *sozo* that comes in Jesus at, of all places, the courthouse. One of the few Veterans Treatment Courts (VTCs) in the United States is right here in Montgomery County; the presiding judge is a friend of mine named Ken Goble. The VTC facilitates an eighteen-month program designed to provide redemptive justice to veterans who have been convicted of crimes. They are given a chance to repent, to turn their lives around before they end up in jail. There is a high degree of accountability and support for everything from overcoming addiction, to anger management, to marriage counseling, to PTSD treatment—whatever is needed. It is a community-based approach designed to set the veteran up for success.

Grace [Church of the Nazarene in Clarksville, Tennessee] has provided the cake and punch for the last several VTC graduation ceremonies, so we've gotten to hear some amazing stories of redemption. One of those came this last Tuesday from a man who'd gotten into deep trouble after serving his country in the Army. As this veteran read his testimony and thanked everyone who had invested in his turnaround, he gave credit to Jesus, in whose name he had been forgiven, restored, and made whole. As this humble man took his seat, the courtroom full of people applauded him. This week the disabled man from Acts 4 looked like a large, bald,

---

6. John Holbert, "A Fresh Wholeness: Reflections on Acts 4:5–12," *Patheos,* April 29, 2012, http://www.patheos.com/progressive-christian/2012/04/fresh-wholeness-john-holbert-04-23-2012.aspx.

Sample Sermon: Steve Estep

black man with tattoos on his forearms. He stood before us having been made well in the name in Jesus.

We don't know what the lame man looked like, but I think I got an email from her a few days ago. Her email read:

Pastor Steve,

My name is Dee. I have been attending Celebrate Recovery for over a year now. I can honestly say it has been a program that has saved me and my marriage from disaster. I am about to finish the step study and will do a testimonial at some point. I can't go into all the details here, but I wanted to thank you for supporting Celebrate Recovery.

A grateful believer in Christ,

Dee

The disabled man in Acts 4 is a soldier who became a Christ follower right here last Sunday; he's the man who stood in Judge Goble's courtroom in a graduation ceremony last Tuesday; he's a lady named Dee who sent me an email on April 17. Each of these people is evidence of Jesus's power to heal, save, and restore. As Christians, we confess that the *sozo* the world needs is found only in Jesus—and we have the evidence of resurrected communities all over the world to show for it. When we call Jesus "Savior," that's what we're talking about.

Every time we come to the Lord's Table, I say, "The body of Christ, broken for us." Most of the time I also say something like, "He was broken that we might be put back together," or, "He was broken so we could be made whole." What I'm really saying is, "He was broken so we could be *sozo*-ed." *Sozo* looks like deliverance from the destruction of sin. *Sozo* looks like reconciliation and the restoration of relationships. *Sozo* looks like a Tuesday afternoon graduation at the Veterans Treatment Court, where lives are transformed and Jesus's name is lifted high. *Sozo* looks like the physical and emotional healing we see at Celebrate Recovery. True *sozo* only happens in the name of Jesus. We celebrate that today with thanksgiving; we experience it today with gratitude. Jesus offers that to all who need forgiveness, wholeness, and restoration. *Sozo*.

nineteen ▪ CONSIDER THE CONTEXT

A word fitly spoken is like apples of gold in a setting of silver.
—Proverbs 25:11

▪ EXEGETICAL work involves not only the biblical text but also the local context—the congregation or community of faith to whom we are preaching.

Rabbi Stacy Offner writes that there is a Hebrew phrase engraved atop the Torah-containing ark before which she stands when she preaches. The phrase is *Da Lifney Mi Atta Omed* ("Know Before Whom You Stand"). She writes, "Those words go through me and challenge me like a prayer. It is my obligation, as a preacher, to know before whom I stand. The words most obviously point to God as the one before whom I stand. But I believe that the power of the words is that they force me to focus as well upon my congregation."[1]

In one of the classes I took in my doctoral studies at McCormick Theological Seminary, Dr. Todd Johnson (who now teaches at Fuller Theological Seminary) shared some insights about how the biblical preachers, particularly in the book of Acts, demonstrate the ways in which exegesis of the congregation can and should influence the proclamation of the Word. In the following six passages, the purpose or desired response of each sermon is the same: each of the preachers announces the good news

---

1. Stacy Offner, "A Jewish Perspective: Pursuing Justice through Knowledge of Self and Others" in *Preaching Justice: Ethnic and Cultural Perspectives* (Eugene, OR: Wipf and Stock Publishers, 2008), 116.

about Jesus in hopes of bringing conversion. However, the circumstances, the context, and the audiences to whom they preach determine *how* these preachers go about it. These preachers knew exactly before whom they were standing, and they structured their sermons accordingly.

Acts 2:22–42

The setting is Peter's sermon on the Day of Pentecost; the location is the city of Jerusalem. Faithful pilgrims from at least sixteen different places listed in Acts 2 are there to celebrate the feast of Pentecost. The Holy Spirit comes in power upon the followers of Jesus who are praying and waiting for the Spirit to arrive. The earth shakes, the wind blows, and the followers of Jesus begin to proclaim the gospel in every language that is represented. As a confused crowd gathers to see what is happening with the mighty wind, tongues of fire, and the sound of Galileans speaking in languages they should not be able to speak, Peter rises to the occasion and preaches the gospel. He is mindful that the Jewish audience will be familiar with David and the Psalms, so he starts on common ground before moving to what they need to know about Jesus of Nazareth. Peter presents Jesus as the fulfillment of what the Jews have been waiting for and what David wrote about. Peter's approach to proclamation is highly context-specific.

Acts 3:12–26

In this chapter, Peter has another opportunity to preach, this time before a crowd after the healing of a lame beggar at Solomon's Portico. Here Peter preaches about Jesus again, but this time, he begins with a confrontation and direct call to repent. But even as Peter blames the crowd for Jesus's death, he couches his language in grace and assumes a pastoral tone: "I know that you acted in ignorance . . ." (v. 17). His approach is much different here than it was in chapter 2, but the gospel message and the call to response are the same. Though the goal of both sermons is conversion, the methodology is different because it is contextualized.

Acts 7:2–53

This is Stephen's speech before he is stoned to death as the first martyr. The audience in this case includes the high priest, the Sanhedrin, and the religious leaders who oppose Stephen. The rhetorical strategy Stephen employs is to recount Israel's story. He preaches about Abraham's call and the covenant of circumcision; he reminds the crowd how Joseph's brothers sold him and God used it for good; he tells the story of Moses and the exodus and speaks of how Solomon built the temple.

Then the story becomes an indictment. Throughout the sermon, Stephen has referred to Israel's rejection of God's messengers, and now he imputes the same sin to his hearers: "You stiff-necked people! Your hearts and ears are still uncircumcised. You are just like your ancestors: You always resist the Holy Spirit! Was there ever a prophet your ancestors did not persecute? They even killed those who predicted the coming of the Righteous One. And now you have betrayed and murdered him" (vv. 51–52). Then the crowd stones him. He wanted them to believe—instead, they rebel.

Like Peter in Acts 2, Stephen started with what his hearers knew and then moved them toward what they didn't know. That strategy can serve as an example for us.

It's also worth noting that these first three sermons from Acts make use of *heilsgechicte*—salvation history. This is a good strategy if you're speaking to people who know the story of God's work in the world; but in our postmodern context, where people may not be familiar with salvation history, we may need to adjust our rhetorical strategy accordingly.

Acts 13:13–43

While Paul and Barnabas are in the synagogue in Pisidian Antioch, the leaders ask, "Is there a word of encouragement for the people?" The audience here is comprised of both Jewish and gentile hearers. Paul takes the lead in offering an encouraging word by giving a brief history of Israel that highlights God's faithfulness. He then tells the story of Jesus, who stands in the line of David as the fulfillment of God's promise to send a Messiah. The word of encouragement is that, in Jesus, there is forgiveness of sins—and the result of Paul's sermon was that many wanted to hear more.

There was never a question about what Paul was going to preach when given the chance: his message would always be Christ crucified and Christ resurrected. But the way Paul presents the gospel is different in

Pisidian Antioch than it is at Mars Hill, and context is what precipitates the difference.

Acts 17:22–34

Here Paul preaches in the Aeropagus in Athens. While walking around the city, Paul observed the Athenians' shrine to an unknown god. In this case, Paul doesn't use Jewish Messianic language; he doesn't tell the salvation history of Israel. Instead, he emphasizes that Jesus reveals the God these philosophers have been searching for. In the end, the sermon moves some people to become followers of Jesus, and it sparks conversation among some of the philosophers. Again, while the message continues to be Jesus, the methodology continues to vary.

Acts 26:2–29

After being arrested, Paul stands before King Agrippa and tries to convince him to believe. Like Peter, Paul opens with an appeal to salvation history and then moves into a personal history or testimony.

In these ways, Scripture offers a model in which the content of the sermon—the good news of Jesus—is the same but is presented differently depending on the context and the audience. As Craig Barnes notes, the ability to know and speak to our local context makes all the difference.

> Pastors . . . have to be well-schooled in over two thousand years of major theological poetry in order to know the gospel truth they preach. And they have to hone their skills as poets in order to present that gospel to their congregations with all of the relevance and life-overhauling power that it had when Jesus spoke to Palestinian Jews in his ancient society. Most seminaries do a much better job of training their students how to do the first thing—knowing the truth. That's what all of the courses on church history, theology, ancient languages, and biblical exegesis provide. It schools students in the major poets. But few new pastors have been trained in the exegesis of a local culture, a particular congregation, or the human soul.

The legacy of this is that we are better at knowing the deep passions and pathos of dead people than the ones we have vowed to serve.[2]

Due diligence; exegesis; consulting the scholars. This is all part of preparing ourselves to preach. Hopefully, by the time you've employed all these different means of engaging the text, you've experienced an epiphany, or "aha" moment. If not, don't be disappointed. Many times I've gone through my entire process only to be left sitting with my head in my hands, still unsure what God wanted to say to or through me. Regardless, there has never been a Sunday on which I was left with nothing to say to the faithful who gathered to hear a word from God.

When the Spirit gives us the first "aha," there is clarity about what direction the sermon needs to go and to what end or purpose. Only then are we ready to move to the second "aha": how to say it. The question at that point becomes: What form will the sermon take? How will it be structured? Will it have points? A plot? Will it be dialogical? Inductive or deductive? Will it start in the text or in modern life? Will it include voices besides that of the preacher? As we mentioned in the chapter on genre, the preacher can and should take a clue about sermon form from the form of the text.[3]

To borrow a musical metaphor, the preacher becomes an arranger at this point. This is not to say the preacher is on his or her own to figure out how to articulate the message. Remember Jesus's words in John 12: the Father told him not only what to say but also how to say it. We see this clearly in the ministry of the prophet Jeremiah.

Jeremiah 13:1–11

God told Jeremiah to buy a linen belt and put it around his waist. God then told him to hide the belt in the rocks until it was ruined by the

---

2. Barnes, *The Pastor as Minor Poet*, 26–27.

3. I highly recommend the following resources for further reading on this topic:

Thomas G. Long, *Preaching and the Literary Forms of the Bible*. Minneapolis: Fortress Press, 1989.

Mike Graves, *The Sermon As Symphony: Preaching the Literary Forms of the New Testament*. Valley Forge: Judson Press, 1997.

Jeffrey D. Arthurs, *Preaching with Variety: How to Re-Create the Dynamics of Biblical Genres*. Grand Rapids: Kregel Publications, 2007.

weather. That linen belt would then serve as the image for Jeremiah's sermon about how God would ruin the pride of Judah. Jeremiah could have preached that sermon without the tattered linen belt—but he didn't. He lingered to find out not only what to say but also how to say it, and God gave him the means for the message.

Jeremiah 18:1–6

The image in this passage is a favorite among preachers: God told Jeremiah to go down to the potter's house, promising to give him a word when he got there. God made good on the promise by using clay to show Jeremiah a picture of what God wanted to do with his broken people. Once again, God told Jeremiah what to say and how to say it.

Jeremiah 25:15–29

This time God told Jeremiah to take a cup representing God's wrath and "make all the nations to whom I send you drink it" (v. 15). Cup imagery in Scripture is powerful. In this case, God has Jeremiah take a bitter cup of wrath to his people. They would have also been familiar with some other cups from the Seder (or Passover) meal. The God serving up wrath in Jeremiah 25 also served the cups of sanctification, deliverance, redemption, and restoration. That same God would also not only provide but drink the cup of suffering and salvation that would become for us a cup of remembrance shared every time we come to the Lord's Table. The sensory element of Jeremiah's message is strong. It is something worth noting in our preparation and proclamation. God equipped Jeremiah not only to tell but also to show. Great preaching today is also a combination of showing and telling.

Throughout his preaching ministry, God told Jeremiah not only what to say but also how to say it. This ranged from "Put a yoke around your neck; buy a field; bury some rocks" (Jeremiah 27; 32:6–44; 43:8–9), to "Have a wine party for the Rekabites" (Jeremiah 35). It was common for Jeremiah's proclamation to involve object lessons, but there was no predicting what he would say or how God would have him say it.

It's unlikely that God will call us to employ the same creative methods in our own preaching that Jeremiah was told to use; nevertheless, Jeremiah's story teaches us that we can trust God to show us how to preach his word in our particular context.

PART 2: WHAT TO SAY

■ ■ ■
Sample Sermon: Love Must Be Given Away
Preached by Tim Whetstone

While serving as chaplain at Point Loma Nazarene University, Tim Whetstone audited a preaching class at Nazarene Theological Seminary, in which much of the material in this book was shared. Tim preached this sermon for his last service as chaplain at Point Loma. It was a unique context and a unique occasion that most certainly impacted what he saw and shared from the text.

2 Kings 5:1–14

It's four years later for many of us, and for some, graduation is incredibly real! I guess the mission statement here is true: "Teach, shape, send." Well, seniors, I'm with you! For many of us, as we journey into the next season of life, the future appears to be filled with ambiguity, uncertainty, even fear. I believe that it's filled with change for all of us. So how will we live in light of this change?

Psalm 24:1 says, "The earth is the Lord's, and everything in it, the world, and all who live in it." I love this verse for many reasons, but it always makes me reflect on one profound and shaping question: "Do I live this way?" Even when the earth doesn't operate as we think, expect, or hope it should, do we seek to live in the promise that we are the Lord's? Personally, I sometimes find it difficult to live in a world where wounds and wonders, life and death, joy and sorrow seem to kiss each other at every turn. Yet is it possible to live in the promise of Psalm 24:1 with gratitude and humility?

As I was preparing for this day and the parting words that would accompany it, I was plagued by the question, "What am I going to preach?" When I prepare to preach, I have what I call a "holy disturbance" come over me as I strive to be faithful in bringing the word and life together. I am humbled in this holy disturbance as I seek to share a word about whose we really are. We belong to a good God, even if our particular circumstances don't seem all that good.

It was in these often tear-filled moments of holy disturbance that the Lord led me back to 2 Kings 5. I've heard hundreds of sermons on this passage but have rarely heard any that concentrated on the character who most captivates me in this story.

Sample Sermon: Tim Whetstone

First, let's recap a bit: It's the fifteenth century BC, and Aram (modern-day Syria) is at war with Israel. Aram has conquered Israel, and as history testifies, wars are never pretty. Syria destroyed Israel: death, destruction, and despair were everywhere. Villages, towns, and cities were demolished. Many Israelites lost loved ones, and those who survived were forced into exile, which included slavery. This entailed a loss of dignity, self-worth, and freedom.

But imagine with me for a moment this particular scene in 2 Kings 5: We're standing in the home (or palace, more likely) of Naaman the general. Here in this room, we encounter two women. The first is Naaman's wife. The second is who I believe to be one of the most often forgotten characters in the story—a young slave girl.

Who is this young slave girl? Why is she even mentioned in the story? Given the context, we can imagine her probable backstory: This young slave girl is Hebrew. She's from Israel, which was taken over by the people she now serves. She's faced the loss of her family, friends, home, and everything else. She's seen tragedy in the form of destruction, bloodshed, rape, and death. And now she has no rights. She is a slave; worse, a female slave; and even worse, a foreign female slave. She has no right to vote, no right to education, no right to own any personal property, and for the most part, no right to even speak in public.

Yet historical research indicates that she probably developed a fairly intimate relationship with her mistress from spending so much time with her. Therefore, in the confines of this room, the mistress may have granted the young slave girl the opportunity to speak. Even so, this anonymous slave girl (we don't even know her name) would most likely have chosen her words carefully. She speaks only ten Hebrew words, which vary from thirteen to seventeen words when translated into English. The New Living Translation reads, "I wish my master would go to see the prophet in Samaria. He would heal him of his leprosy" (v. 3).

Really? That's it? She could have said, "Ha ha! That's what you get for being a general in the army that took my homeland!" But she says nothing of the sort. What's wrong with this girl? Or rather, what's "right" with this girl?

I once heard author, speaker, and family life educator Larry Henshaw tell a story about when his daughters were young and the family lived in the coastal California area. One day, while Larry and his wife were in one part of their house and the girls were playing in another room, an earthquake struck. It was strong enough that Larry immediately ran to the girls to help get them to safety. However, when he reached their room, the door was shut. He tried to open it to no avail. The door was stuck—some furniture had slammed up against the door and was blocking it.

Unable to open the door, Larry called out to the girls, "Are you all right?" But he heard no answer—just gasps of fear. So he called through the door, "Hey, girls, remember, you're Henshaws. And Henshaws don't need to worry right now because everything is going to be all right."

There was a long pause. Finally, from the other side of the door, one of the girls spoke up and said, "Yeah, Daddy . . . I think we take after Mommy's side of the family!"

So here in 2 Kings, we have this anonymous slave girl (history would indicate she is probably a young teenager) who lives differently than most of us do today. Who remembers who she is?

First, she remembers whose she is! She remembers "which side of the family" she takes after; she remembers that she is a child of Yahweh. Her circumstances don't dictate her family identity. The same is true for us. There is nothing—not an education, title, job, or institutional affiliation—that can change our family identity as children of God!

Second, the slave girl remembers that she is loved by Yahweh. She may have endured loss, tragedy, and enslavement, but none of that changes God's love for her. God does not love her because of what she did or did not do. God *is* love—and because God is love and loves first, God loves her not based on performance! The same is true for us. God's love for us is not dependent on our performance; his love does not change with our circumstances. God gives love, and we receive love!

Third, in remembering and receiving Yahweh's love, the slave girl knew that this love was not hers to keep. True love cannot be hoarded; it must be given away! Freely we received, and freely we give! This young, anonymous slave girl is remembered not for her accomplishments, awards, or prestige but for giving love to someone who's hurting in a different way than she is—her mistress.

Naaman's wife is also facing life-altering circumstances: her home, friends, and way of life will change. Her husband will lose his position, and

Sample Sermon: Tim Whetstone

they will be forced to live outside the city gates. And she will likely lose him to this life-threatening disease.

But with ten Hebrew words, the young slave girl speaks renewed life into this woman's wounded heart. This young girl is present and points beyond herself to a place of healing! She serves out of love. Crazy, right? And because we don't even know her name, all the glory truly goes to God!

As many of us leave PLNU together, I'd like to encourage us all to live in the same way as this young slave girl. We too can point beyond ourselves. In the power of the resurrection and through God's Holy Spirit, we can live pointing beyond ourselves to Jesus Christ!

Will it be easy? Not at all. In fact, this is often the harder, more dangerous path. The young girl in our passage obviously didn't have an easy life. Yet whatever season of life we are traversing, we can live our lives pointing beyond ourselves. In fact, I believe we are called to such a life—even Jesus lived this way on earth. In the Gospel of John we see Jesus pointing beyond himself to the Father: "These are not my words; these are not my works; these are not my miracles; this is the Father who has sent me. And if you have seen me, you have seen the Father. So you've seen how the Father would have us live. Therefore, 'as the Father has sent me, I am sending you'" (20:21).

As we are sent daily by the Son of God, may we be those anonymous kingdom agents who point to the one who has sent us! As you do so, may you be encouraged. Remember that you are a child of God; you are always loved; and the love you receive is meant to be given away.

Martin Luther King Jr. shared these words with his own congregation in one of his final sermons. Death was on his mind, as was the question of how he would be remembered for living. He shared the following words with his congregation at Ebenezer Church in Atlanta, Georgia:

> If any of you are around when I have to meet my day, I don't want a long funeral. And if you get somebody to deliver the eulogy, tell them not to talk too long. Every now and then I wonder what I want them to say. Tell them not to mention that I have a Nobel Peace Prize, that isn't important. Tell them not to mention that I have three or four hundred other awards, that's not important. Tell him not to mention where I went to school. I'd like somebody to mention that day, that Martin Luther King Jr., tried to give his life serving others.

I'd like for somebody to say that day, that Martin Luther King Jr., tried to love somebody.[4]

As I leave you all today, I pray that you remember that I tried to love somebody, to give my life in service to others, to point beyond myself to Jesus. Thank you, my dear kingdom family.

---

4. Martin Luther King, Jr., "The Drum Major Instinct," (sermon, Ebenezer Baptist Church, Atlanta, GA, February 4, 1968). https://kinginstitute.stanford.edu/king-papers/documents/drum-major-instinct-sermon-delivered-ebenezer-baptist-church.

twenty ▪ INCLUDING OTHER VOICES

■ LISTENING to other pastoral and theological voices in the process of preparation is a common practice. Get a group of preachers in the same room and it won't be long before the conversation goes that direction. We preachers like to talk about what we do, and most of us also like to hear about what our colleagues do and how they do it. There are many ways to incorporate other voices into our process. We can consult podcasts, Lectionary groups, online forums, or local church study groups.

I mentioned previously that I am not the only one involved in my process of sermon preparation. Over the years, I've had the privilege of serving alongside some incredible pastors on our staff. Prior to our weekly staff meeting, we all do the same work with the text. Sometimes it is in reading each other's initial observations that the "aha" moment comes. A comment becomes a conversation that lights a fire in everyone in the room. That's when it becomes obvious that we've hit on not just an interesting discussion point but also a direction for proclamation. Sometimes this direction comes from one of my observations, but often it comes from someone else at the table.

The concept of a group approach to sermon preparation may be new to you; it was to me when I first started doing it in 2003. Prior to that, my sermon preparation was primarily a solitary task. Occasionally I might discuss a text with one of my pastoral colleagues, but for the most part, preparing to preach was a solo affair.

That changed during my doctoral program, when one of my assignments was to form a parish project group (PPG), which was a group of laypersons who walked through the process of preparing three sermons a year. The PPG changed from year to year, but after listening to the first group's insights, observations, struggles, and joys with the text, I was hooked on a process that involved voices besides my own. From that point on, sermon preparation became a communal practice for me.

The process of preparation I've described in this book can certainly be performed individually; I have done it myself countless times. But I would encourage you to at least experiment with inviting other voices into the process. A communal process of preparation can be a valuable experience not only for you but also for your congregation—especially those who sense a call to ministry themselves.

At the end of the day, no one else should tell us what to preach or how to preach it. God has specifically entrusted us with the call to preach and to prepare; it is unacceptable for us to defer these responsibilities to others. However, it is also true that some of the best ideas, insights, and images I've encountered have come from my co-laborers in this process. There is no substitute for the inspiration of the Holy Spirit, but sometimes the Spirit speaks through the voices of other believers.

All of this takes time. It takes time to write down initial observations and listen to the insights that others bring to the table. It takes time to look for bad news, good news, universals, and the image of God in the text. It takes time to reflect on what responses would be appropriate to the text. And it takes time to do the work of biblical and congregational exegesis. But what we are doing in this process is preparing for a significant event when God's people gather around the Word and Table. Typically, we do whatever is necessary to prepare for significant events—may it be so with our preaching as well. The call to preach is the call to prepare. Sometimes the best preparation happens in community.

Sample Sermon: The Active Mission of Jesus
Preached by Mike Jackson

The following sermon was preached by Dr. Mike Jackson at Clarksville Grace Church of the Nazarene in Clarksville, Tennessee. Mike is the professor of preaching at Trevecca Nazarene University and filled the pulpit when I was given a two-month sabbatical. Mike was also exposed to the PPG process as a student in his doctoral program and continues to implement it. He involved a group of people in the preparation process for this sermon and invited them with him into the pulpit. They did not physically stand before the congregation, but their observations, insights, questions, and contributions were shared as the sermon unfolded. Mike gave credit where credit was due, and the process of inviting and involving other voices gave shape to the content and form of the sermon.

Luke 8:26–39

For years I read this text as a beautiful, powerful story of the transforming power of Jesus Christ in a person's life. The contrast in this man's life could not be more striking! Consider the difference an encounter with Jesus makes in this man's life:

Before/After
Naked/Clothed
Lived among tombs/Back to the city
Bound with chains/Free at last!
Wild and screaming/In his right mind
Falling down at Jesus's feet/Sitting at Jesus's feet
Begging Jesus to leave/Begging Jesus to stay

This is clearly a story of God's power to deliver and transform—right? But then I read this passage with a group of laypersons at my church, and they ruined the story for me! If you want a fresh, dangerous, world-changing encounter with the text, read it with other people. They will ask interesting, probing questions you never thought to ask.

First, Lois asked a disturbing question: "Why does everyone *beg* Jesus to leave after he performs this amazing work of healing? You would think they would ask Jesus to stay and do more miracles—not leave." Now that's a good question!

It makes sense that the people were upset about losing their pigs, especially if swine farming was the primary means of survival in this community. It reminds me of the story in Acts 16 about the slave girl who made her masters lots of money by telling fortunes. But when Paul set her free from the evil spirit that held her captive, the girl's masters were furious because their means of making money was gone! So maybe the Gerasenes were angry that Jesus upset their economy. Make no mistake: when Jesus comes into your life, he will mess with your money—and lots of other things too!

Maybe a more fundamental reason why the Gerasenes asked Jesus to leave is that people don't like change. We like our world to be comfortable, familiar, and predictable. Change terrifies us. I remember how Luke describes Peter's first encounter with Jesus in 5:1–11. After Jesus helped him bring in a miraculous catch of fish, Peter was terrified at the power of this rabbi. His reaction makes sense. If Jesus has this kind of power, it's the end of the world as we know it—and that is terrifying!

All I know is that Lois asked a good—but disturbing—question. If this is simply a tale of Jesus's power to heal, why do the people beg Jesus to leave? Perhaps there is more going on here than a simple story of healing.

Then Alan asked a simple question that forever rocked my reading of this text. He asked, "Pastor, where is this country of the Gerasenes?"

Being a well-educated seminary graduate, doctoral candidate, and resident Bible expert, I answered, "I have no idea! But I'll look into it and report back to you next week."

During my research into this simple question, I made an earth-shattering discovery: this is the only time in Luke's Gospel that Jesus sets foot in gentile territory. Gentile territory is the land of aliens, outsiders, unclean people. This is enemy turf. This is a land of tombs and graveyards. The stench of death is everywhere! Speaking of stench, did you notice that this place is also filled with dirty, stinking pigs? Everything about this land screams, "Unclean! Stay away! Holy people, do not enter here!" Which raises a question: What's a nice Savior like you doing in a place like this?

Several years ago, my friend John served as associate pastor in Topeka, Kansas, at a church that was literally on "the other side of the tracks." He and his family lived in the old parsonage next door to the church, and many nights they woke to the sounds of sirens, gunfire, and screams. It was a neighborhood filled with gang warfare, drug trafficking, prostitution, and violence. When another pastor drove by the tracks with a visiting missionary, he told the missionary, "We never go to that part of town."

What?! If we don't go there in God's name, who will?

Finally, Jim made another disturbing observation. The healed man begged Jesus to let him stay and become his disciple, but Jesus said no. That seems a little harsh—after all, this man was a new convert. He had not yet been trained as a disciple. He needed a loving community to nurture him in his faith; he would not make it back in pig country on his own. If there was ever someone who needed to spend time with Jesus, it was this guy!

But Jesus refused his request, saying, "Return to your home, and declare how much God has done for you" (8:38, ESV). At this point, thanks to Lois, Alan, and Jim, my eyes were opened to the realization that this is not so much a healing story as it is a mission story. This man was Jesus's first missionary!

An encounter with the mercy and grace of Jesus does more than help you clean up your life so you can sit at Jesus's feet clothed and in your right mind. It means more than joining the holy huddle, studying the Bible, and becoming a sanctified, growing Christian. It's a call to join Jesus in full partnership in the mission of God.

Ours is the story of a God who took on human flesh; a God who got his hands dirty; a God who dared to go into gentile territory, the land of death. "What's a nice Savior like you doing in a place like this?" The answer is simple: Jesus is bringing God's healing love and saving power to the darkest and most broken places of our world.

This has always been God's *modus operandi*. Our God is always working on the other side of the tracks, coming all the way to pig country, getting his hands dirty with human affairs. He heeds the cries of Egyptian slaves and uses his strong hand to set people free. He uses the prophet Elisha to bring healing power to a Syrian army general—once again, working on the other side of the tracks and blessing those we would call enemies. And when the Word becomes flesh, Jesus keeps showing up in all the wrong places too: partying with tax collectors, hanging out with prostitutes, welcoming dirty, rotten sinners of all sorts.

One thing's for sure: it's not easy to follow a God like this! And so this text gives us both a promise and a warning. The promise is this: If your life is bound up and broken, Jesus has come to set you free. He gives peace to the brokenhearted; freedom to those held captive; life to those who are as good as dead. If you're looking for a fresh start, you've come to the right place. But the warning is this: To follow Jesus is to go with him into pig country and join him in his mission!

Who will share God's love with the lost and broken people of Clarksville? Who will go to the places of suffering, pain, and alienation to be the body of Christ broken for them, the life of Christ poured out for them? Who will dare go into gentile land (where the sinners live), to pig country (where the unclean dwell), to the other side of the tracks (where good, respectable, churchgoing folks do not go)?

If *we* don't go in God's name, who will?

There is one thing I am sure of: when we do finally get over our fears and go to these places, we will find Jesus already there, working in the margins, loving the unlovable, embodying the good news of God's love and mercy to all who are lost and broken.

My invitation today is twofold:

1) Do you need Jesus's healing touch in your life? He has truly come to heal us, to save us, to deliver us from our brokenness. His promise to us is life, joy, forgiveness, healing, and peace. Is that what you're seeking today? Come to Jesus. He is faithful; he is good; he is mighty to save.
2) Have you been a spectator in the Christian life? To follow Jesus is to join him in his mission of loving and healing a broken world. The good news of what Christ has done in your life is meant to be shared with your neighbors. Will you offer your whole life to God and join Jesus in his mission of love and compassion to a lost and broken world?

twenty-one • LONG-RANGE PLANNING

■ **HOW MANY** times have you have felt pressured this week as you wondered how you could possibly get everything done? I have found that planning, praying, and working ahead are necessary actions to preserve my own sanity and prevent heart attacks, ulcers, and mediocre sermons (not to mention a miserable spouse and kids).

Years ago I received an email from a fellow pastor. It was written for leaders in the business sector, but some of the content is applicable to our own work of preparing to preach:

Why Planning is Indispensable

In preparing for battle I have always found that plans are useless, but planning is indispensable.

—Dwight D. Eisenhower

As Supreme Commander of the Allied Forces in Europe during World War II, Dwight D. Eisenhower planned, coordinated, and carried out the largest amphibious assault ever undertaken—the Invasion of Normandy. Historians regard him as one of the greatest military strategists of all time. Even so, Eisenhower considered plans to be essentially worthless.

Eisenhower was no fool. While he recognized that concrete plans would sooner or later be discarded in the course of battle, he prized the process of planning. Why? Because he knew firsthand the benefits it could bring.

[. . .]

1) Planning Prepares You Mentally and Emotionally

When planning, you walk down the avenue of possibilities in your mind. This exercise mentally familiarizes you with the pros and cons that may be associated with the decisions you make. Also, projecting yourself into the future acquaints you with some of the sacrifices that will be necessary to see a plan through to completion. Oftentimes, being aware of these costs in advance helps a leader to prepare emotionally to make tough choices.

2) Planning Helps You to Prioritize Your Resources

Opportunities abound, but you can't do everything. Planning helps you to separate what you *must* do from what you *could* do. By prioritizing, you more effectively allocate precious resources of time and capital.

3) Planning Causes You to Identify Assumptions

As any mapmaker knows, a good roadmap must be drawn to scale and must have a legend explaining its symbols. Without these two essential features, the map is confusing and unreliable to the reader.

Assumptions serve as our legend and scale when we map out a path for those we lead. We really can't make a sensible plan for the future until we've defined our assumptions. Planning exposes assumptions to the light of inquiry. When considering a future plan, we have to test whether or not our present assumptions remain valid. This process helps us refine our fundamental beliefs about the mission, values, and goals of our organization.

Summary

Plans are disposable. As such, perhaps it's best to write them on recyclable paper, but never stop the discipline of planning. Although a majority of your plans will end up being abandoned and discarded, the process of planning won't fail to reward you.[1]

---

1. "When Plans Don't Go According to the Script, Keep Planning," The John Maxwell Company, updated June 11, 2011, http://www.johnmaxwell.com/blog/when-plans-dont-go-according-to-the-script-keep-planning. (Emailed to me by Tommy Vallejos, August 24, 2009.)

Many of the benefits of planning outlined in the article also apply to preaching. When it comes to developing a long-range preaching plan, I would also add the following benefits:

1. Saves time—if we don't spend time deciding on a text every week, we can begin engaging the text sooner.

2. Helps those who are planning the other aspects of the service—music, drama, the sacraments, video clips, etc.

3. Helps us intentionally provide a balanced diet of Scripture to our hearers.

4. Prevents us from preaching "at" people or issues.

5. Lengthens our preparation time—we may gather insights, stories, or images in the months to come that we can later add to a sermon.

6. Enables us to promote sermon series and special days in advance.

7. Lowers the preacher's stress level (and the stress level of those around us).

So how do we go about long-range planning? Every year, I take a few days with our pastoral team to develop the year-long preaching calendar. I am primarily a Lectionary preacher; the three-year Lectionary cycle provides both flexibility and continuity, and I have found it to be very beneficial. And while I will occasionally change things up by preaching a series that is not Lectionary-based, I do still follow the Christian calendar, which provides a cadence for congregational development in the faith. Prior to the planning retreat, I or another staff member will develop a document that lists the dates for every Sunday of the year along with the corresponding Lectionary text; this becomes the primary calendar from which we work.

I'm sure that I am a Lectionary preacher because those who have been most influential in my approach to preaching have practiced Lectionary preaching. I want to share a few of their quotes to encourage you to consider Lectionary preaching. But we'll begin with a bit of a disclaimer statement from Leonora Tubbs Tisdale: "Lectionary preaching, as valuable as it is, also needs to be tempered by congregational concerns in the text selection process. Indeed, slavish adherence to any preset preaching program—Lectionary or otherwise—militates against genuine contextuality."[2]

Walter Burghardt says, "I advise preachers, whenever possible, to base their sermons on the Lectionary. Why? Because such preaching is more likely to stay close to God's revealed Word, follow the gospel story through a whole liturgical year, and compel the preacher to link today's human problems to Scripture."[3]

Barbara Brown Taylor says, "I have been a Lectionary preacher for so long that I fumble when I have to pick a text out of thin air for a special occasion. When I pick the text, it seems that I am shopping for a piece of Scripture that will back up what I already know I want to say. When the text picks me, I know I am in for a discovery. The Lectionary provides me with breadth and discipline I lack on my own, and my sermons are fresher with it than without it. The liturgical year provides a natural pattern for preaching."[4]

Robert Farrar Capon says,

I tell you this . . . in the hope that if you are leery about preaching from the Lectionary (or even if, like many preachers, you use it but sit loose to its texts when they don't grab you by the throat in the first two minutes), you'll be encouraged to get over those bad habits. Man proposes, God disposes: all you have to be when you settle down to any text is *disposable*. With a preacher who's willing to sit dumbly at the feet of Scripture like Mary at the feet of Jesus (Luke 10:38–42), God can do great things. It doesn't matter if you haven't got a clue to begin with. Sit there and hang out with the passage that stumps you. If God has anything he wants you to say next Sunday, he'll get it said. His Word is already present in the words themselves. Let *them* speak to you, and the Word himself will speak through you."[5]

---

2. Tisdale, *Preaching as Local Theology and Folk Art*, 101.

3. Thomas G. Long, "Patterns in Sermons," in *Best Advice for Preaching*, ed. John S. McClure, (Minneapolis: Fortress Press, 1998), 41.

4. Ibid.

5. Capon, *The Foolishness of Preaching*, 72.

While the Lectionary is a useful tool, there are other options available to preachers who seek to develop a long-range plan. But before we get to those, a few words about calendars.

When most people are asked to make plans, they'll say, "Let me check my calendar."

For preachers, however, life is not so simple; we are obliged to say, "Let me check my (multiple) calendars!"

First, there is the *liturgical calendar*: Christmas and Easter, Advent and Lent, Pentecost and Epiphany—each season and festival brings its own themes and demands on the preaching task.[6]

In his book *Sabbath*, Wayne Muller addresses how following the Christian calendar connects us to the larger church, past and present. "The liturgical year grants us this pearl of great price: *You are not going anywhere. Millions have done this before you, and millions will do it after you are gone. When you drink this cup, light this candle, recite this prayer, there is sacredness and magic in it. It is a gift for you, to help you remember who you are, and to whom you belong. Come, and take your rest.*"[7]

Whether intentionally or by default, we preachers serve to form and inform a congregational rhythm, or cadence, that can be either ordered and purposeful, or disjointed and chaotic. Long-range planning can add purpose to the corporate faith formation that happens through preaching. Some may view observance of the Christian calendar as optional, but as far as I am concerned, a Christian understanding of the ordering of time is essential for preachers who want the year of sermons to work together to create a sense of purpose. As William H. Willimon writes:

> We are not redeemed *away* from time but as Paul says in Galatians, God moves *into* time, adopts our time, redeems us from bondage to time's ravages, and generates 'the fullness of time.' That's the

---

6. If you are unfamiliar with the Christian year, I would suggest a few resources: Laurence Stookey's *Calendar: Christ's Time for the Church* and *The New Handbook for the Christian Year* and Bobby Gross's *Living the Christian Year*. All three resources are very helpful when trying to get a handle on the liturgical, or Christian, calendar.

7. Wayne Muller, *Sabbath: Finding Rest, Renewal, and Delight in Our Busy Lives* (New York: Bantam Books, 1999), 90.

main reason the church attempts to take time in the name of Jesus demanding that we follow the church year. The church teaches us to mark time according to Epiphany, Lent, and Easter rather than the Fourth of July, Thanksgiving, and Mother's Day. We are thereby encouraged not to escape time (as in some Eastern religions) but rather to live in time as those who know what time really is."[8]

The *ecclesiastical calendar* brings an array of denominational and church-related events. Many churches observe and participate in things like stewardship season, theological education Sunday, race relations Sunday, World Communion Sunday, mission emphases, Faith Promise Sunday, and more. In the Church of the Nazarene, the ecclesiastical calendar is often associated with special offerings for a variety of Nazarene-specific programs and institutions, like alabaster, Nazarene Theological Seminary, Nazarene Bible College, The Foundry Publishing, and more. The ecclesiastical fiscal calendar may or may not align with the January-to-December calendar year, so we should also pay attention to year-end and new-year issues that may impact the preaching calendar.

The *civic calendar* includes public holidays like Thanksgiving, Independence Day, Martin Luther King Jr. Day, Mother's and Father's Days, and more. Sometimes the preacher will have to decide which calendar to honor: for instance, what will we choose to emphasize when Mother's Day and Pentecost fall on the same Sunday? Civic holiday weekends usually also carry their own implications for church attendance, so an emphasis that is intended to generate momentum or financial giving would be ill-placed on a historically low-attendance Sunday. As you go about your long-range planning, paying attention to the civic calendar can save you some disappointment.

One civic calendar we should always have nearby is the school calendar. In the school district that was part of my church's community in Clarksville, Tennessee, there were week-long fall and spring breaks, as well as significant time off between Christmas and New Year's Day, which are factors every preacher should take into consideration when planning

---

8. Willimon, *Undone by Easter*, 9.

a series or special Sunday. We put on the preaching calendar things like, "Last Sunday before school starts" so that we can pray for the teachers, administrators, and students before they start a new school year. Graduations and other significant events are also noted.

Finally, there is the *local church calendar*. Every congregation has its own docket of anniversaries, homecomings, festivals, and program emphases that deserve recognition in worship, and sometimes in the sermon.[9] If you're a preacher with some tenure, the local church calendar has probably been ingrained into your rhythm already; if you're coming into a new church context, it's wise to get familiar with the local church calendar as quickly as possible.

Take a few days to work on a long-range plan, and take all of your calendars with you. Consider using one of the following approaches (list adapted from Thomas G. Long in *The Witness of Preaching*):

1. *Lectio Continua*—This approach involves preaching straight through the Bible or a particular book of the Bible. The methodology is straightforward: If you preach chapter 1 this Sunday, you start with chapter 2 next Sunday. The preaching plan moves verse by verse, chapter by chapter, book by book. There are some advantages to this approach. You know where you're going from week to week; the congregation knows where you are going and can read ahead and develop their own questions. It is easy to make this approach holistic by using the same texts for small groups and weekly Bible studies. This approach thoroughly immerses people in one book of the Bible at a time.

2. *Lectionary*—The Lectionary provides a list of Scriptures corresponding to the various days of the church calendar in a three-year cycle. Readings are set to the rhythm of the church year and typically include an Old Testament, Psalm, Gospel, and Epistle passage. These are often tied together thematically and can lend themselves to a homily that interweaves multiple texts. One advantage of this approach is the number of great resources available in print and online. The growing popularity of

---

9. I drew heavily from Long's "Patterns in Sermons" in *Best Advice for Preaching*, 35–36 for this discussion of calendars.

the Lectionary makes it possible for preachers to participate in Lectionary groups with pastors from other denominations, which can broaden our understanding or experience of a text.[10] The downside of the Lectionary is that, even in a three-year period, some texts are not addressed at all.

3. *Local Plan*—In this approach, the preacher develops their own local church Lectionary, either alone or with the help of a committee. A local plan can be a good idea if it includes a broad spectrum and intentional balance of scriptures. The downside of a local plan is that it lacks the broader support and resources of the Lectionary.

4. *Preacher's Choice*—The preacher selects texts based on the pressing needs of the moment, usually on a week-to-week basis. The advantage of this approach is that it's easy to preach with passion when you're addressing the issues that are most pressing in your own spirit. The danger is that the preacher may gravitate toward particular texts and themes. Consequently, the congregation may not receive a balanced diet of Scripture.

5. *Mixture or Combination*—Another approach to long-range planning could incorporate a combination of Lectionary or local plan for certain seasons of the year, then move to particular emphases or sermon series during Ordinary Time.

Whether you choose to preach *lectio continua*, the Lectionary, local plan, preacher's choice, or a mixture of any of these, the benefits of long-range planning apply across the board. A few days of prayerful planning can eliminate hours of struggle throughout the year and enable you to maximize your preparation time.

---

10. Lectionary groups with pastors from other traditions often reveal or expose the biases, preferences, and limitations our chosen theological tradition inherently brings to the task.

AFTERWORD

■ I BET you still remember the first sermon you preached. When we recall our first sermons, it's easy to feel all over again the initial and overwhelming inadequacy, angst, and dependence we had on God as we prayed, pried, and maybe even cried in a desperate attempt to hear a word from God so we would have a word for God's people.

Over time, the sense of desperate dependence on God can become an underwhelming, Spirit-less, been-there-done-that routine that results in a lack of fire in the pulpit and a yawn in the pew. Overfamiliarity with the holy can create a presumptuous approach to proclamation; it can turn sermons into academic exercises or moral lectures. When that happens, our preaching fails to do what Augustine said it should: delight, inform, and persuade. Why is that? How do the passion, excitement, and sense of utter dependence on God fade away? How does the task of preaching ever cease to drive us to our knees and then rise with the boldness that only comes from having heard from God?

There are several ways we can lose sight of the gravity of our call. We can become lazy. We can look too much to outside sources before looking to God for sermon content. We can become pimps of the Word, overconfident in our own abilities, or overfamiliar with our sacred responsibility. We can get frustrated that people don't seem to remember the content of our sermons as much as they remember what they want to criticize about the way we deliver them, our administrative skills, how much time off we took last year, or how our children misbehaved last week.

The demands of pastoral leadership take a toll, and one of the places it's most likely to show is in our preaching—and, more specifically, our preaching preparation. It is here that preachers are tempted to resort to quick fixes. The abundance of information at our fingertips makes it all too easy to shape our sermons around the work of other people before we engage the text and spend the time it takes to hear a fresh word from God.

    The tools and strategies in this book have been offered in the hope that they will deepen your relationship with Scripture and with the God of Scripture. My prayer is that you who are called to preach the gospel will never be satisfied with bringing a word that has not first taken root in you—so that the lives of your hearers might be redeemed, restored, and transformed by the living Word whose message we are privileged to proclaim. There is no higher calling than to embrace this humbling role of preaching the Word of God in defining, potentially transformative moments. These meaningful moments call for our best preparatory efforts—so get yourself ready.

www.ingramcontent.com/pod-product-compliance
Lightning Source LLC
Chambersburg PA
CBHW070120100426
42744CB00010B/1881